SEAGRY'S BEST 2000 PHOTO A... SEAGRY KNOWLEDG... EVER

Jack Staveley

...nah.B Barney Vowles Class 2.

ss2 Florence age 7 Ben Parsfitt year 3

Book Neil Shortorne class 2 Age 7 Jonathan Holtsock Photographs year 3

...otographs and Book of seagry photos O's

...n about Seagry 2000

...ry Yasmine

class 3 year 4 The Greatest memories of 2000

...raphs S. Helena Harry cool photoers in Seagry School and village Grace Watling

KALEY watt year 3 class 3

...gry school our jolly 2000 photo Best boo...

village

...phs George Nash year 3 Reece Clark 3

Reflections of
SEAGRY

A Wiltshire Village Bids Farewell To The 20th Century

The final year in pictures - photographed by Paul Stallard,
words by Tristan Cork

A limited edition of 1000 copies to mark the Millennium

First published in the United Kingdom in 2000
Candid Pictures 6 The Courtyard Seagry Chippenham Wiltshire SN15 5JZ

Hardback limited edition published 2000

Copyright: Paul Stallard & Tristan Cork

All rights reserved. No part of this publication may be reproduced, stored in a retrieval system, or transmitted in any form or by any means, electronic, mechanical, photocopying, recording or otherwise, without the prior permission of the publishers and copyright holders.

Website: http://www.seagry2000.fsnet.co.uk
E.Mail: stallard@tesco.net

ISBN 0-9538822-0-9

Type: Palatino 10pt
Front cover design: Paul Stallard

Typesetting and origination by
Paul Stallard and Tristan Cork

Printers: Hackman Print
Cambrian Ind. Park, Clydach Vale, Tonypandy, Rhondda, CF40 2XX

Printed and bound in the United Kingdom.

Contents

Foreword...........................page 5

Introduction......................page 6

Introducing Seagry....................page 7

The Final Year Of The Century Begins.........page 15

Spring..................page 23

Summer...............page 47

Autumn..................page 103

Winter..................page 119

Acknowledgements...............page 128

Foreword

The village is one of the most interesting ways of understanding modern England. But it is not as simple a picture as all that. Our countryside never was the arcadia of popular myth: a smiling land full of cakes and ale, gaffers and gumboots, wenches and wassails.

The truth is much more complex, but all the more rewarding to unravel. So we must congratulate *Paul Stallard* and *Tristan Cork* for the skill and care they have brought to this fascinating book.

In a world full of audio-visual miracles: film, video, tape, internet and so on, it might even be thought too simplistic to try and capture the life of one village in words and photographs. The reverse is true. These brilliant shots that Paul has collected over the cycle of a country year are more eloquent and memorable than the restless images that chase each other over our screens day and night. Together, they make up a chronicle of frozen moments that will speak to future generations as moving pictures cannot. They are admirably complemented by Tristan's cool, sensitive prose. It's at once obvious that both young men have won the trust and goodwill of the infinitely various men and women who inhabit modern Seagry.

Their book was put together at a time of appalling crisis for the English countryside. Farming as I write is facing a major catastrophe; it's clearly reflected in these candid pages. The collision between town and country over issues like hunting is also reflected; as indeed is the simple but fundamental question of how much more urban life can encroach if the village is to survive. The coming of the motorway is a curse or blessing, depending on your view point. It has deprived Seagry of its sleepy past for ever; but it has brought a corridor too, from which the new generation of villagers can make their assault on prosperity and promotion in the cities, while still enjoying village life.

And the traditional cornerstones of village life thrive in Seagry still: an active church, a busy hall, a lively pub, and a most impressive school. There are moments of drama, as the international rugby footballer Eric Peters shatters his knee on the eve of the Five Nations and World Cup; there are moments of romance as three very different Seagry couples marry; there are moments of hope, as we contemplate the cheerful faces of the village's youngest inhabitants - the ones who will inherit this fortunate corner of England one day.

They are indeed lucky to have this enchanting record of how it felt to live here as the new Millennium dawned.

Godfrey

Former Editor of the Sunday Times Magazine: *Godfrey Smith*, Malmesbury, June 2000

Introduction

The idea for this book was born on a warm summer's evening over a couple of cool drinks - the birthplace of so many dreams and schemes - most of which do not survive the dawn! This one however, not only survived but materialised into the object in your hands.
Paul Stallard had the original inspiration to create a photographic record depicting life in his home village of Seagry at the end of the 20th Century - possibly for an exhibition. A book project soon became the result of the logical progression of Paul's vision, and the willing co-operation of his friend and colleague, Tristan Cork, was enlisted to write the words.

Work began in January 1999 and the Parish Council subsequently endorsed the project as the official Seagry Millennium celebration. The objective was to produce an illustrated chronicle of a small North Wiltshire village preparing to enter a new Millennium. A book to appeal not only to lovers of rural life but to provide an interesting social document for future generations to enjoy.
Acknowledgements appear elsewhere, but the enthusiastic involvement of members of the village community has been considerable and cannot be overstated, not only in providing the material for the book but in supporting on-going fund-raising ventures to meet production costs.

Finally, Seagry has been singularly fortunate to have Paul Stallard, a creative and talented photographer living in the village at this historic moment who together with fellow journalist, Tristan Cork, have both devoted a great deal of their spare time and energy to this enterprise.
Without their dedication and professionalism .... Enjoy the book!

Derek Kemp

Illustrations
Front cover: *Images from around the village.*
Title page: *Images from the four seasons.*
Contents page: *Royston Ball driving his vintage Lanchester through the listed gates of Seagry House.*
Previous pages: *Through the gate on the eastern edge of Oak Hill Wood. And the entrance to Seagry from the west taken in the Autumn.*

Introducing Seagry

WHEN this tree survived its first winter, the surrounding countryside didn't look too different from today. As the thousand years have passed, the tree has seen most of its neighbours cut, woods have been cleared, large open fields were enclosed into a patchwork of smaller fields, then hedges were cleared to make large fields again. But the surviving woods from which the seed came are still thick and dark around it.

From the top of this ancient tree, the geography of Seagry spreads out to the east. The tree stands near Seagry's highest point, the village sits on the true edge of the Cotswolds. To the west, the countryside becomes much more Cotswold-like: little mellow stone villages like Kington St Michael and Castle Combe are interspersed with hollow valleys and rolling hills. But the change from Cotswold to clay is barely noticeable. The eastern edge of the Cotswolds is just a gentle slope down to the River Avon, which winds lazily along the wide and beautiful Dauntsey Vale. With Seagry, and therefore with this book, you get two villages for the price of one. Upper Seagry sits on the higher ground on the edge of the gentle hill, Lower Seagry nestles around the church on the north west bank of the Avon.

Man has looked out on the view from where this tree now proudly stands for thousands of years - an artefact from the Upper Palaeolithic Age, early Stone Age to you and me, has been found in the village.

The oak at Scotland Lodge is probably the only living survivor from the last time the people of Seagry prepared for a new Millennium. Instead of fears over computers going wrong, the eve of the year 1000AD brought with it very real fears of more invasions from the north. A thousand

years ago, Seagry stood close to what was the border of two countries - Wessex and Mercia. As the 10th century drew to a close and our tree began to grow, almost constant battles raged between the Saxon armies and the Danes, who had already conquered Mercia.

But it was with a great deal of hope and optimism that Seagry went into the final year of the second Millennium. Some things change, some things looked like they'd never change, but the tree at Scotland Lodge remained impassive.

FOUR buildings make up the four cornerstones of community life in Seagry. Like many villages, it has a pub, The New Inn, a historic church, a village hall and a village school.

The school used to be on the corner of the road to Lower Seagry and the main Great Somerford Road which has always formed the divide between Upper and Lower. Built like almost every Victorian village school, it looks more like an old church than a modern school. But the early 60s brought with it a rise in the school roll and a new, modern school was built on land at Upper Seagry. When more of the Victorian village schools were closed in the following years, including at nearby Rodbourne, an extension was built and now Seagry School is one of eleven village primary 'super-schools' in the Malmesbury area, with pupils from as far afield as Corston, Somerfords, Malmesbury as well as Seagry itself.

North Wiltshire villages have either one of two

Previous pages: Upper Seagry (left) from the air, with The Knoll in the bottom left corner and the school playing field in the centre. Lower Seagry (right) grew away from the church (on this page, above), with Trinity Farm dominating the village.
Right: The New Inn, taken from The Knoll

kinds of village halls. They are either modern, functional, brick and stone buildings, built after years of campaigning and fund raising. Or they are older, original village halls, made of whatever came to the hands of the volunteers between the wars - wood, corrugated iron, prefab materials. Draughty and with a temperamental water supply, these village halls are slowly being recognised as unpolished gems of rural life.

Seagry and Startley Village Hall fits into the second category - not least because of its illustrious past of mixed fortune. During the first world war it was used as a studio in the garden of Rookery House in Lower Seagry. The Countess Gleichen, a painter, and her sister, a sculptress, used the hall until new owners turned it into a chicken shed.

Then, Lady Cowley, who lived at Seagry House, bought it and held a fete to raise funds for fitting the building out as a village hall. Since then, its role has remained unchanged. If there's an event of any size, it happens in the village hall. It's home for the parish council, the pre-school group and various clubs and meetings. It's being continually improved by a dedicated band of volunteers and plans are being made for an extension.

The New Inn has existed for well over a century,

and survived the rash of village pub closures when the clamp down on drink-driving came in the last 20 years or so. Now, in common with most pubs, it is equally, if not more, a restaurant than a traditional drinking pub.

The final year saw the first major change in a decade. The landlord of 11 years, Dave Lock sold the pub to new owners, but the pub remains as a focal point for evening activity in the village.

The church of St Mary the Virgin looks older than it actually is. Like most parish churches, the myth among lucky tourists who stumble across it down the no through road, and villagers alike, is that the church was built some time during the Medieval period, and has remained virtually unchanged ever since. Seagry church is a good example to blow the myth: it was largely rebuilt in just five months of 1849 and had been continually tinkered with from its early Norman origins, tinkering which continued well into the 20th century.

What is for certain is a church has stood on the site at Lower Seagry for at least 900 years, and probably much more than a thousand. On higher ground with the historic village around it, Seagry church was, from the 1180s to the time of the dissolution in the 1540s, administered by Bradenstoke Priory, which overlooked the Dauntsey Vale from its lofty position on the top of the escarpment just a few miles to the east.

This would have set Seagry slightly apart from its neighbouring villages, all of whom would have, to a greater or lesser degree, been overseen religiously and therefore politically by the famous abbey at Malmesbury.

Nevertheless, when the dissolution came, and Bradenstoke Priory was disbanded, Seagry Church experienced mixed fortunes. Some decades saw enthusiastic vicars, living in the heart of the village and respected by all - other decades saw absent vicars, who were based sometimes many miles away, and would pay young and inexperienced, or old and unenthused clergy to deal with the bind of the weekly service. The Church of England suffered mixed fortunes too, in the final years of this century, but in Seagry reports of its death are more than premature.

During the 1980s, Seagry parish found itself joined with neighbours at Great and Little Somerford, Corston and Rodbourne; Rev Guy Oswald, who arrived in the area in 1982 and took

> *'The hall was used as an artist's studio until new owners turned it into a chicken shed...'*

Top: Seagry and Startley Village Hall. Right: Contrast the architecture of the former Victorian school house (top) with the present Seagry School, built in the 1960s.

over Seagry in 1987, watches over a large rural flock.

No background to Seagry would be complete without mentioning what has slowly become the most important change to the village in the late 20th century.

The effects of a decision to build a six-lane motorway on the southern boundary of the parish are still being felt in 1999, even though the first cars sped past almost 30 years ago.

The Dauntsey Vale tapers to a point at Wootton Bassett in its north east corner, and here the M4 motorway rolls over the top of the hill and descends into the Vale serenely.

It crosses the Vale from north east to south west, crossing the River Avon on the edge of Seagry's south east boundary. Within weeks of the first sight of the bulldozers on the horizon, Seagry found itself cut off from its nearest southerly neighbour, the village of Sutton Benger, and only a new, wide road bridge connects them now.

Left: While there aren't quite as many horses as people in Seagry, this one, owned by local farmer Robert Dickinson, is curious of the camera on a glorious spring day in Seagry.

But more crucially than the physical presence of a motorway a stone's throw away, was what the road builders constructed near the next village west - Stanton St Quintin.

The 17th junction of the motorway on its route from London to Bristol and South Wales suddenly brought Seagry much closer to the rest of the country - and brought the rest of the country closer to Seagry.

From then it took just half an hour to get to Bristol and just an hour and a half to arrive in London.

While this was great news for those villagers who had lived in relative isolation in a sleepy corner of North Wiltshire, it meant that suddenly it could be possible to live in a rural idyll like Seagry and yet still work in a large city many miles away. This was to have implications that would change the village, its people and its community forever.

But this book, like the villagers it will show, will not seek to look back.

The final year of the Millennium was used by many as a time to rewrite the history books, or to dream of what the future would hold.

This is neither. This is quite literally a snapshot of life in a typical village in rural England at a time of momentous changes yet still unmoveable certainty.

We hope the book will grow more valuable as the 21st century unfolds. In 50 years' time, we hope it will be the kind of window on the past we wish we had now.

The Final Year of the Century Begins

THE FINAL year of the century began, as many a year before had, with Seagry and its people at the mercy of the weather. The rain came down hard and fast during the first weeks of 1999. It ran off the Cotswolds and slowly the River Avon became swollen and murky. The town of Malmesbury, five miles upstream and based on an iron-age hill top site surrounded by the two main branches of the young Avon, almost became an island once again, and the water spilled over the banks and out into the Vale.

Here at Seagry Mill, the fields became lakes in the weak January sunshine, the river became a torrent and on one night in particular, sandbags were filled earnestly.

But the morning brought clear skies which stayed until this picture of a gloriously damp winter sunset. The rain abated, the river flowed on to flood Chippenham instead, leaving villagers to get on with the rest of the winter with dry feet and a reminder that although it might be a momentous year, nature knows no numerics.

WHILE the wildlife and landscape seem to go to sleep, it's the ideal time to do some major pruning. Once a year, local farmers hire a man and his machine to trim the roadside hedgerows, while villager Dermo Selwood, below, gets to grips with a hedge at the village school. For a couple of weeks afterwards, the village loses its natural charm and feels rather shorn, but it has to be done. Leave it any later, and the wildlife of spring will be damaged.

SIXTEEN years of living in Seagry hasn't dampened Bill Cardno's enthusiasm for his Scottish homeland, and on one night of the year - Burns Night at the end of January - he can truly celebrate all that is Caledonian.

For the first time, The New Inn staged a special Burns Night event, with the traditional dish of haggis, 'neaps and tatties - turnips and potatoes to us Wiltshire folk.

The haggis was ordered down especially from Scotland and everyone ate what was on the menu, which also included traditional Cockaleekie soup.

Bill is pictured here, glasses off for extra passion, addressing the haggis before it was devoured.

Apart from the lone Scottish accent among the Wiltshire voices in the village pub, the night followed the pattern across the country and in Scotland, with one exception: Not surprisingly, there is always a distinct shortage of bagpipe players in Wiltshire, but on Burns Night...

So, pictured below, a fiddler was drafted in to give a slightly Celtic air, filling in at the moment the haggis was supposed to be piped in.

If 1999 saw big changes in the relationships of Scotland, England and Wales (Tony Blair's government brought in devolution), the union seemed to be strengthened in Seagry.

For not only was Burns Night a successful first for the village pub, but St David's night, St Patrick's Night and St George's Night followed during 1999 with equally traditional national grub.

The New Inn Shooting Club. Clockwise from the top left: Derek Kemp, Dave Clark (Snr.), Phil Thomas, Dave Clark (no relation) and Dave Tucker, Nobby Lewis and (centre picture) Dave Lock.

TWO village pastimes, at opposing ends of the noise spectrum. The New Inn Shooting Club meet every fortnight, either on land at Trinity Farm in Lower Seagry, or in a disused quarry in nearby Stanton St Quintin.

With a regular membership of around ten, and a full complement of nearer 18, the group shoot nothing more lively than a fast-moving clay disk.

It brings together villagers, mostly men but also a few women, in an informal yet slightly competitive test of skill and aim.

Each member pays £10 a shoot, which covers everything from the cartridges and clays to the surprisingly high cost of insurance.

Pictured here, in early February, organiser Nobby Lewis, is pictured on the bottom left, manning the trap, the machine which sends the clay pigeon soaring.

In the village hall, however, a cold and dark night is livened by a Beetle Drive.

It's organised by Mary Lewis on behalf of and with help from the church; young and old enjoy the simple pleasure of rolling dice, and drawing the body, head and legs of a beetle, according to the number thrown.

Like bingo, the first to complete their beetle shouts 'beetle!' and everyone changes seats, just in case no one knows each other, for another round.

Younger 'drivers' bring along coloured pens - there are prizes for the 'best-dressed' beetle.

IT'S NOT just the village hall that welcomes and warms villagers on a dark, winter evening. Many a freezing February night has been chilled by the cut and thrust of a quiz night at the New Inn.

A school teaching couple, Andrew (right) and Avis Ball set the questions, harvested from a forest's worth of encyclopedia and fact books.

The winners in 1999 retained their trophy from last year. Jim and Ann Stent, who moved to the village from London recently to live next door to Uncle Doug Wiltshire, teamed up with Anne's sister Helen Ballard and husband Mike, (*pictured below right*).

IT WOULD be a cliché to pick someone as a 'Mr Seagry', but *Michael Lewis* would have a pretty good case should someone force the issue. Known as 'Nobby' to everyone except his wife Irene, the chairman of the parish council lives, eats, breathes and sleeps the village he's called home for 50 years.

He moved to Seagry at the age of eight - his father was demobbed and got a job at Trinity Farm in Lower Seagry. The family moved to one of the three workmen's cottages, having previously lived in Idover, near Little Somerford, Callow Hill, near Brinkworth and Braydonside. He followed his father's muddy footsteps to a job at Trinity Farm, played football and cricket for the village teams, and became a county-standard football referee.

Like many post war young men, Seagry offered as little in the way of social activity as it does now. One of many trips to the infamous Tarantula coffee bar in Malmesbury proved fruitful, and he met local girl Irene, who hadn't even heard of Seagry. The incredulous suitor had to show her his driving licence to prove such a place existed only four miles down a country lane.

Three children and six grandchildren later, the couple are still very much involved in Seagry life. As well as the chairman's duties, Nobby helps organise the New Inn clay pigeon shooting club, was chairman of the cricket club, and along with Dermo Selwood, helped to organise 1999's fireworks display.

If there's something to get involved with in Seagry, Nobby Lewis will be there, and 1999 was just as eventful as many a previous year of village events. There was the time in February when his hair was shaved in aid of the BBC charity fund-raising drive Comic Relief, the Millennium Eve Party in the village hall and the village's entry in the Best Kept Village Competition.

"Somebody's got to take a lead in the village," he says.

THE YEAR *Doug Wiltshire* moved into his house in Upper Seagry, the General Strike took over the country, and no one had heard of Adolf Hitler. It was 1926, and 73 years later Doug still doesn't feel the need to move. Seagry is his home.

Born down the road in a house called Polkerris, his father was head groundsman at Hungerdown House, in the days when big houses had even bigger staff. After leaving school aged 14, Doug worked for eight and a half years for his dad, despite suffering an accident, which cut off the fingers of one hand. That ruled him out of seeing any serious action in the looming world war, Doug spent a 'quiet' one making aircraft parts in Swindon, and doing maintenance work at nearby Hullavington aerodrome. After the war there wasn't much money in gardening, Doug remembers, so he settled down to work as a maintenance man at a gravel pit in Christian Malford.

One of 16 children, 13 of whom survived infancy, Doug has never married, never been abroad and has lived for most of his life with brother Fred. In 1960, Doug embarked on the little task that has made him Seagry's most celebrated resident. He began to cut the grass outside his house. Over the years, the area Doug and his mower has covered has gradually increased. The improvement was noted, and

whenever local newspaper reporters come, wanting to know why Seagry consistently wins the Best Kept Village title, grateful villagers point them in the direction of Doug's door.

As well as the verges, Doug has lent a hand to the cricket pitch and the village hall, although he's quick to point out his acclaim should really be for the village as a whole. "Seagry is the kind of place where a few people do a lot of work. The Selwood family, for instance have never had the credit they deserve over the years."

Doug's contemporaries have all but gone, although each morning for 50 years, he has called in to Manor Farm to see childhood friend Bill Hayward. The final year saw Doug leave a lasting mark on the village. With the help of John Kingston, he planted an oak tree on the Knoll, which will be there well into the next century.

*Above: When the snowdrops, pictured here on Seagry's cricket field, begin to turn, you know that the winter is almost over, and that soon it won't be woollen clad sheep patrolling the outfield but woollen-clad fielders.
Below: The club asked local smallholder Eric Barnes to graze his sheep on the field - they are much cheaper and more thorough than any lawn mower.*

Spring

THERE is probably an old English saying to suit all possible ways in which winter becomes spring, but no one could think of one to describe the way it happened in 1999. Winter gradually warmed into spring, perhaps a little earlier than when it was supposed to. Daffodils heralded the milder weather as always.

In Seagry, it's not just the lack of frost on commuters' cars or noticing you don't see your breath anymore in the mornings that tells you it's spring. For the village is surrounded by woodland, meadows and lush damp fields, which are home to an abundance of wildlife, from deer, hares, rabbits, buzzards, badgers and swans to domestic creatures like horses and even the odd donkey.

Spring is celebrated instinctively in a rural community like Seagry, perhaps even without the people knowing quite why.

Traditions like the Easter Bonnet Parade at the village school hark back to a time when the onset of spring meant the difference between life and death for the people and their animals.

Now, spring is still a time when the whole village seems to awake, bursting with activity, new life and new hope.

IF one thing symbolises Spring, it's the new life brought to church with a christening. The full parish records don't begin to show how many thousands of babies born in Seagry through the centuries have been carried, unbaptized, up the path to the church, to be brought back as a member of God's family.

For Lydia Catherine Clark's big day, the April showers stayed away, the sky was largely blue although it was quite 'brisk', remembers proud father Alastair.

Rev Guy Oswald presided over the service at Seagry Church. "Guy is very good, and doesn't mind holding a special private service for a village christening," said Alastair.

Around 40 guests, close family and friends, attended the christening, on Sunday, April 18, and then went back to their home at Scotland Lodge on the outskirts of the village.

Young Lydia, five months old on her big day, was

Seagry's youngest resident at the turn of the year, joining elder brother Reece, and big sister Verity.

Above: Guests arrive at the church; Below: Alastair, Vanessa, baby Lydia and Rev Oswald

24

CHARITY events are as important as ever in 1999, and the one that gets the most involved is the BBC's Comic Relief appeal.

One Friday in early spring, it seemed everyone donned red noses and fancy dress and took part in madcap challenges to raise money for the needy in both the developing world and here in Britain.

Above and above right: Children at Seagry School had as much fun as anyone, with six-year-old Robynne Hinkley as Ginger Spice Geri Halliwell standing out.

Right and below: New Inn regulars Nobby Lewis and Phil Arnold before, during and immediately after their head shave in the pub that night.
Not only did it raise £482.50, it also inspired the parish chairman's new look. He kept it short for the rest of the year

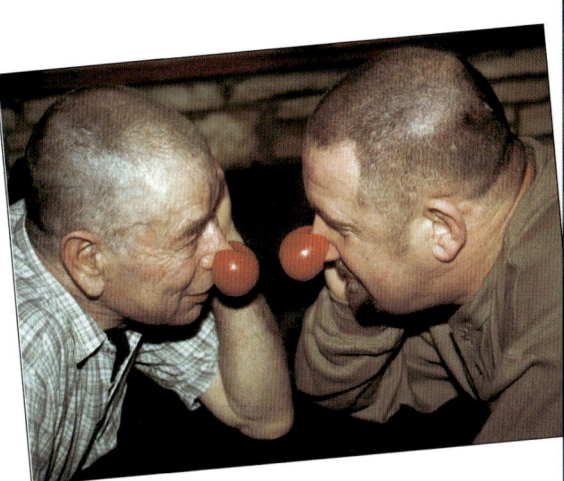

NO ONE saw the crisis which engulfed the farming industry during 1999 clearer than *Eric Barnes*, for not only has the father-of-three got eight acres and two dozen ewes in Seagry, but he also is proud to know hundreds of farming families from Chippenham to the other side of Gloucester.

For Eric is the man who sells the feed to the farmers. He has around 600 farming families on his books, but reckons in the last few years, he's seen half that number fall by the wayside, as farmers give up, sell their land to their neighbours and turn their farmyards into executive development.

Farming is in this man's blood. He was raised in the Dorset village of Critcheldown, which became well known after a famous legal wrangle between local farmers and the Ministry of Defence. His passion is speedway, and that was where he met Audrey, a farmer's daughter on holiday from Coalpit Heath near Bristol. The pair were married within 18 months, and Eric, who had already worked as a farming salesman for seven years, arrived in Gloucestershire to take up a new challenge. He reckons to know personally almost every farmer in his massive patch of rural Wiltshire and Gloucestershire, and sells feed and seed worth a quarter of a million pounds a month. But times are hard, and Eric has noticed the difference. "If it carries on like this for another year or so, there'll be widespread bankruptcy. Thirty herds have gone in the last two years that I trade with. At Chippenham and Gloucester Markets, there's half the farmers there were, and whereas they used to be buzzing, lively places full of laughter, now there's long faces everywhere and it's like a morgue. Each time I go there, there's a farmer giving up and selling . But I still manage to put on a new account a week." The last year of the century was 'one of the worst yet' for Eric's farmers.

Back home in Seagry, Eric and his wife Audrey tend to their flock. When they lived in nearby Corston, 20 years ago, they had pigs. Does he ever feel the need to have cows? "No," he jokes. "They're much too much hassle!"

THE NINETIES will go down as the decade of 'downshifting', and *Richard Bridge* is unashamed of following the trend. For the former City businessman swapped life as the chief executive of a plc in April 1999 for the role of managing director of a jigsaw company in rural North Wiltshire. Richard did the ground work for this 'downshift' - a term describing how the City Whizzes of the greedy 80s jacked in their fast-paced deals and moved to the country for the quiet life - early. In 1991 the family moved to Lower Seagry. Wife Harriet is a local girl and the family had many friends in the area. "It's great here, I really do love every minute of it. My old friends from the City come down and say 'how the hell did you get this?' They've all got this idea they've got to get out. I am lucky in that this is extremely satisfying."

But the carefree life doesn't appeal to Richard. He turned the Pinkney-based Wentworth Jigsaw Company from a £132,000 loss to a £13,000 profit in just nine months, and says he worries just as much if not more about his new role.

"We employ 12-15 people and they really care about what they do. When you're sitting on top of a great big pyramid, you never really see the whole picture. Here you're actually making something and we don't have room for a bad six months. But I'm good under pressure."

It was a year of change for the former merchant banker; instead of wheeling and dealing, he found himself personally delivering jigsaws to Prince Charles' Highgrove House, and overseeing production of a jigsaw commemorating the wedding of Prince Edward to Sophie Rhys Jones.

Back home, and the family has noticed the difference. "I used to kiss goodnight to my daughter Sophie on a Sunday evening, go off to work and not see her again until Saturday morning," he says ruefully. As well as her dad being around much more, 1999 was a good year for the 11-year-old too - she won a scholarship to nearby Grittleton House School. "It's the quality of life," he smiles. "You can't put a price on that."

A FORTIETH wedding anniversary and an encounter with a brother he'd never met before - 1999 was quite a year for Derek Wakefield.
The former bus driver married Primrose Duckett on March 28, 1959 at Kington St Michael Church just a couple of villages away from his home in Seagry.
Forty years later, and the same date found them returning from an idyllic Ruby Wedding Anniversary holiday in Lake Garda and Venice in Italy. On their return, there was a surprise waiting. "We turned the corner and there was bunting all over the house," said Primrose. "All our three children were there as well as lots of family and friends."

Among the guests at the surprise party was Douglas White. "Derek has always known he had a brother, who was adopted when he was two. His mother told her children that he was adopted by a family and taken to Canada and that they shouldn't try to find him. But this year, he found us, and he'd been living in Swindon all his life. It was incredible."
Without doubt, after 40 years of happy marriage, Lady Luck has shone on the Wakefields: Their coach trip to Italy involved an overnight stop in Chamonix, in the French Alps. The next day, they went to Italy through the Mont Blanc Tunnel. The next day after that, two dozen people died when the tunnel caught fire.

The village school Easter Bonnet Parade. Above: Nathalie Clarke and Robynne Hinkley. Left: Joseph Kidner. Below: Sophie Robinson, Helena Baker, Hannah Sharpe, Joseph Kidner, Nathalie Clarke and Sebastian Parfitt.

The school has held an Easter Bonnet Parade for as long as anyone can remember. The Friends of Seagry School give Easter eggs to everyone who brings a home-made bonnet in, and the parade followed singing and musical entertainment, and was accompanied by a cake stall and Easter egg raffle, inevitably to raise funds for the school.

Right: Where there was grey and dull brown, now all is an explosion of spring green: The Knoll on a gorgeous day in late April.

THE FINAL year of the century will definitely be one *Eric Peters* will remember.

After a very successful season helping Scotland to their first Five Nations title for 10 years, the Bath and Scotland rugby player found himself at home in Seagry a little too much for his liking after a freak injury left him watching team mates on the telly rather than being in among them.

For the first three months, it had been his best season to date. The big number eight captained his country and was looking forward to the climax of the Five Nations Competition, then the Rugby World Cup when he took the field on April 2 as captain for Bath in a crunch game against league-leaders Leicester.

Ironically, photographer Paul Stallard chose that game to take these action shots of Seagry's rugby hero. Eric, captain for the match, played well and was on hand when Leicester's flying England full back Tim Stimpson broke through with just six minutes to go.

"I tackled him and his knee hit my knee. He was pumping his legs very quickly and we collided. My knee just shattered. I looked down and thought 'oh, no!'. I didn't feel an amazing amount of pain, but I was just gutted because I was six minutes away from the Five Nations and the World Cup and all that. I pretty much want to forget the rest of 1999."

The knee was operated on a day later, and Eric, who began 1999 by celebrating his 30th birthday, spent the rest of the year limping, with the hope he would be back on the pitch to complete the 1999/2000 season.

Born in Glasgow of Scottish parents, he was educated in Essex and began playing for Bath when he left Cambridge University in 1993. He started living in Bristol, then Bath, and moved to Seagry in January 1997 when his wife Katie got a job in Reading.

"We thought it was a nice little village, close to the motorway, and it was halfway between our two employers," he said.

A full-time rugby player, Eric found he had more time in 1999 to return to his other trade - chartered surveying - and worked at King Sturge in the investment team. His wife, Katie, at the start of the year began work at Dyson in Malmesbury.

Above: Eric Peters leading out the Bath side on that fateful day in April.
Top Right: Running with the ball at the Leicester opponents, and Bottom Right: In the thick of the action.

A GOOD barometer of the changing season comes with the stunning floor covering of bluebells in the woods around Seagry. Depending on the season the woods at Seagry are blessed with hosts of the fairytale coverings, normally in late April or early May.

The woods on either side of the Upper Seagry to Stanton road are easy to access. On the left (Ellwood) provision is made for walkers with many footpaths though most bluebells grow close to the road and are interspersed with wood anemones and wild garlic.

In Oak Hill Wood (on the right of the road) most bluebells are near the road at the top (Westend) of the wood and at the peak time are a carpet of blue best viewed on a sunny day. On both sites, walkers can sometimes spot the rarer whitebells.

Above, left and below: Oak Hill Wood on the last day of April

THE OLD joke is that postmen have to be quick on their feet to escape the jaws of snap-happy dogs on their rounds. And it doesn't help that *Jim Whale*, a Seagry resident of 28 years, has a rumbustious Springer Spaniel named Whistler - other dogs on his round in Chippenham town centre often pick up his scent as well as the sound of the letter box opening. But Jim, who turned 52 in 1999, isn't sluggish on his feet. For in April he ran the London Marathon for the second time, completing the 26 miles 385 yards in the respectable time of three hours and 32 minutes.

He finished in about 6,000th place in a field of 40,000 and ended up with exactly the same time as his first run around the streets of the capital.

He started running seriously, as opposed to running from canines, relatively late in life - at the age of 47. A friend of the family was tragically paralysed from the neck down on his birthday while being given the bumps, and along with a few friends, Jim offered to complete a charity run to raise money for his care.

The postie was hooked, joined the Chippenham Harriers and no dog has caught him since.

Chippenham-bred, he arrived in Seagry in the early 1970s because wife Barbara, a country girl at heart, wanted to move back to the country and their cottage was the only house left in their price range.

"It's a lovely village, the people are...lovely. The village hasn't changed that much, although it's surprising how many new people are coming in," he said.

The one consolation with the early starts as a postie is the early finishes - it leaves time for hobbies and the active life. As well as the running, Barbara has a horse stabled at Calne, they play squash at Melksham - oh, and they've got a speed boat in the garage, which often gets wet off the coast of Poole and in the Lake District. One Whale drives and the other does a spot of water skiing. Then they swap over.

IF THE village is known for equine pursuits, one Seagry villager has been flying the canine flag for almost two decades. *Sheila Park* celebrated her 40th year as a Seagry resident during 1999, and at the age of 69, still cares for and breeds dogs.

The little-known breed of dog called a Pomeranian, known for its sharp-pointed face and an abundant coat, has been bred at her home in the village since the early 1980s.

Sheila showed at Crufts every year for 16 years and one dog in particular, known as Little Miss Brodie, or Brodie for short, gained 18 championship tickets in just one year.

Sheila arrived in Seagry from Lacock as her late husband, Raymond, landed the job of gardener for Mr Barnes at Hungerdown House next door, and she has seen many changes in the village since then. "It was all very quiet back then, and then the motorway came and the road at the end of my street was altered."

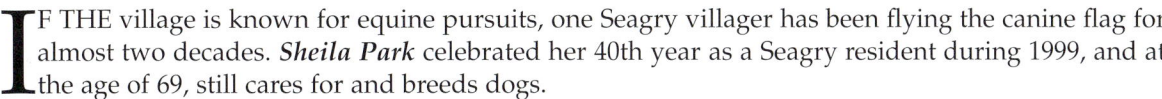

"All these houses were built in Seagry and many of the farms have gone. The village's community feel has changed. All the older ones who would be involved have gone, and new people have moved in, but in time, this will be a lively village as the younger ones tend to be more outgoing."

Many people largely ignored the significance of the change of Millennium, but surrounded by her dogs and largely content, Sheila hopes the dawn of a new century will bring changes. "I hope there will be more peace, and people will be healthier and happier. The last century really was horrific with all the wars. Let's hope it all dies down and the world can settle down to a peaceful time with less greed - money does not get everything."

Seagry's economy is not as dependent on the state of the farming industry as it was, which is probably just as well. The kind of shocking downturn that began in around 1997 with the BSE crisis and continued throughout 1999 with regular cuts in the price of milk would, in decades past, have threatened the very future of the village.

As it was, farmers, their workers and the myriad of associated support industries, all gulped when they thought of the prospects in the new century. One of the problems farmers have is that no matter what the state of the industry, work must go on - several farmers from the village took part in demonstrations and blockades of the 'big bad' supermarkets and dairy firms, often until three in the morning, and yet still had to be out to milk the cows at six.

Seagry's biggest farm is Trinity Farm, which lies on the lush flat ground bordering the River Avon at Lower Seagry. It's land almost designed for turning grass into milk, and 190 Holsteins are milked twice a day.

The Biggin family moved from a farm in Wickwar in 1984 to the 400 acres of prime Dauntsey Vale. For 14 years or so, life was good, but in the last two or three years, the markets have virtually crashed.

The price of beef fell by 30 per cent in one day in 1997, when scientists finally confirmed a link between the brain disease that had been sweeping the nation's cattle for a decade, and a strange and fatal new brain disease in humans.

Trinity Farm has 150 beef cattle, with many more at the other, smaller farms in the village. But if farmers getting out of beef production were hoping for a better time in other avenues, they were to be disappointed. In 1999, the price a Seagry farmer could get for a litre of milk was cut by around seven pence, leaving most farmers at the end of the year with the situation that it would cost them more to produce a litre than they could sell it for. But twice a day, the cows still need milking.

The cows on Trinity Farm have their diet monitored more closely than a health-obsessed Hollywood actress. From October to March they're kept indoors, the nutritional content of their special feed checked by computer. During the summer, the rye grass of the fresh outdoors keeps them producing milk, but through the winter they're fed on forage maize and silage which is grown, cut and prepared on the farm itself.

"A lot of people think you just let a cow out to eat grass and then milk it," said Rob Biggin. "But cows are creatures of habit and it doesn't happen on its own. It's surprising to know that their milk yield actually goes down around ten per cent when, in late March, they're let out onto the fields. We fed them well through the winter in the nice and warm."

Left: Silage making at Trinity Farm, with Nobby Lewis in the driving seat.
Above: Eric Barnes shears one of his sheep, helped by daughter Judith.
Above left: Cow and calf at Nables Farm.
Below: John Biggin on his tractor.

Above: A new arrival for Eric Barnes' flock. This lamb pictured at just ten hours old, tipped the scales at a whopping 12lbs. Eric still uses those old scales for weighing out the sheep's feed, and still wears that 24-year-old jacket. Remarkably, the wool that made the jacket was more expensive then that it is now. Sheep farmers are also feeling the pinch, a fleece could fetch £2.50 twenty years ago, now Eric will be lucky to get 60p.

Left: But the markets don't concern Robert Dickinson's beautiful foals, gambolling as all foals should, in their paddock. Spring also means a host of other new arrivals. Top: Half of Mimi May's litter of Weimaraner puppies are pictured here, while Gordon Ridout tends to a beef calf on Nables Farm (above right)
Above Left: Lucky the kitten was born to one of the cats at Trinity Farm, but its brothers and sisters and mum either died or abandoned it within hours. Found by Nobby Lewis, it was taken in by his wife Irene, and spent 1999 in pampered luxury at Broadleaze.

THE CRISIS claimed casualties across the country, and Seagry was no exception. These dairy cows followed a long line of milkers farmed from Manor Farm, right in the centre of Upper Seagry. But the second cut in the price of milk in 1999 was one too many for John Kingston, who started selling them off in September. Within weeks, 65 dairy cows were gone, and nobody was left milking in Upper Seagry for the first time in probably a thousand years. The lucky ones went to other herds, the unlucky ones, including the last five heavily pregnant cows, went to the burner. John and his wife Rosemary, whose family has farmed in Seagry for almost 80 years, obtained planning permission to build several homes on the site of the dairy unit, and the 100 acres of Manor Farm is left with just 60 or so young beef calves and some arable land.

"We're lucky because we own the land," said John. "We might lose a bit of privacy with the houses next door, but if you're tenanted farmer, you've got nothing to fall back on."

Below: England's blue and pleasant land, a linseed field on Robert Dickinson's land.

The role of farmer's wife is traditionally one of quiet support and hard work, but for *Liz Biggin*, it's a lot tougher than that. For the wife of Rob Biggin, who runs Seagry's biggest farm, Trinity Farm, is also a mother-of-four, parish councillor and runs the farm's administration.

Her life is based around the traditional farmhouse kitchen, complete with Aga and clay-tiled floor that serves as an office and a meeting room as well as a kitchen to cook the family meals,

And Liz could easily stake a claim to have a tougher job than Rob - not that they're competing - given the amount of paperwork now associated with keeping a cow. Each animal requires more forms and documents than her four children require to be registered human beings. Each cow has its own 'passport' - a book running to 50 pages, each its own little form - and Liz has a filing cabinet stacked with 340 of them. Then there's the computerised feeding system, the quota regulations, the subsidy forms and the deals with the dairies. In July, Liz gave up her part-time job as a secretary/PA at a host management company in nearby Startley to become Rob's personal assistant.

She married Rob when the family worked a farm near Wickwar in Gloucestershire, before they moved to Lower Seagry in 1984. Her father-in-law, John, has since taken a bit more of a back seat and is 'enjoying not having to get up at six each morning'.

The extra workload provided by the increasing red tape means Liz can't get involved as much in the community as she used to. She was on the parent-teacher association at the village school for four years when her brood attended, and gave up the chair of the village hall committee in February after 12 years (the baton was passed to a surprised Clare Clilverd in the New Inn that night).

The final year of the century began with an annual treat for the Biggins. The Beaufort Hunt met in their farmyard for their traditional New Year's meet. An avid hunt follower, Liz rode as often as she could, but after a bad accident involving two of her daughters, Trinity Farm no longer has horses.

After the New Year meet, it seemed nothing would stop the new government from banning hunting, while at the same time the government watched as the price of milk fell through the floor. Rob now goes on protest blockades, while Liz tries to balance the books and keep the Aga warm.

IT DOESN'T bear thinking about what the village of Seagry would have missed out on had jobsworth district planners won their 19-month battle with *Derek Selwood* and prevented him from building his own house next to the school in the mid 1970s.

Married to Joy for 26 years, everyone knows Derek as 'Dermo', it's a nickname given to him aged 13 by schoolfriend Tubby Wootton which just stuck. He went to work at Presteel in Swindon with his two brothers so the nickname continued into his adulthood.

"I get to a stage where people say 'Derek' to me and I don't answer - I don't realise they're talking to me. In this village the only person who calls me Derek is Margaret Collins."

Dermo's list of jobs and achievements for the village is impressive and incredible. He does it by choosing to start work at 5.30am and being home by mid-afternoon. During 1999, he completed a seaside garden, as well as continuing to act as general handyman-cum-gardener-cum-football pitch marker at the school.

A parish councillor aged just 18, Dermo has always been quietly doing things in the village. Most of the village hall has, at one time or another, been repaired by Dermo's hand, he ran a successful youth club for many years as well as a youth football team in Brinkworth. The father of two is a school governor, has been on the playing field committee since 1966 at the age of just 16, and spent 12 years on the village hall committee.

"You get to the stage where you're doing too much, with too many fingers in too many pies and you can't do it all. People say you're stupid and you can't say no.

"Now I've forced myself to restrict myself. What I do is a hobby, and I don't mind doing it. It doesn't bother me to go one year to the next without a thank you, it's just a habit I got into."

FOR 18 years, Ernie Darch has presided over democracy in Seagry, and 1999 was as busy as any year before.

There were two elections in the village, one in May to send a representative to the district council in Chippenham, and another in June to help to elect a member of the European Parliament in Strasbourg, on behalf of the whole South West.

There would have been three elections, but only the seven existing parish councillors stood for the council - there was no need for a vote.

Opposite: Farmer Robert Dickinson began planting linseed in the early 1990s. This field, on the western approaches to Upper Seagry is normally planted in late March and early April, but in 1999, the warm spring meant the crop, on 90 acres around the village, went in earlier. The linseed flowers with this glorious purple colour for just a week or so, here mid June, is harvested in mid to late August and the pods are crushed and the oil extracted. There are only two linseed oil crushers in the country, meaning it's cheaper for Robert to send his crop to Belgium.

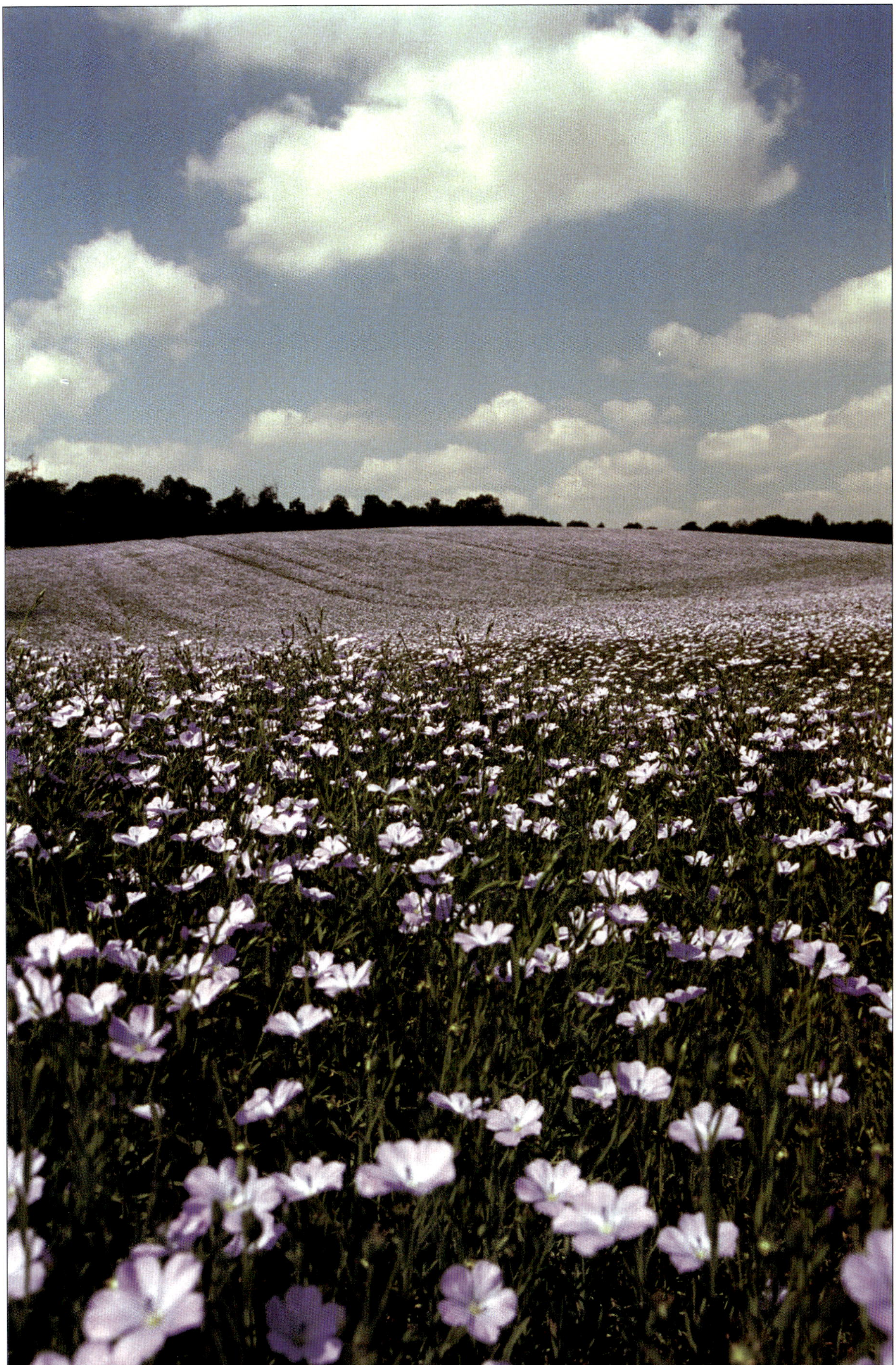

They love their animals in Seagry, and the photographer is no exception. Allowed one indulgence, this is his beloved hound Marley, taking a stroll through the bluebells *(above)*.

Lucky the kitten got out of the pint pot and is now secure with its eight remaining lives with Irene Lewis *(left)*.

Some pets are just too big to keep indoors. So it's just as well this donkey *(below left)* lives on Eric Barnes' smallholding with sheep for company.

And Seagry wouldn't be Seagry if horses didn't get a look in: Kate Winter and her horse *(below)*.

Animals of all shapes and sizes and besotted humans: Cat-lover Isobel Edwards (left); Kathie Stallard has a passion for horses, well served in horse-mad Seagry. But Kate Wykeham's favourite thing is to indulge in a spot of synchronised pig feeding. Today's delicacy: Polo mints.

Seagry is one of eight village schools that have banded together to form what's known as a 'cluster' - pooling resources, expertise and providing the odd shoulder for each other to cry on.

The schools: Christian Malford, Kington Langley, Stanton, Great Somerford, Hullavington, Sutton Benger and Sherston also compete on the playing fields. For the first time for many years, they brought their finest netballing girls and footballing boys to Seagry for the cluster's version of the World Cup,

— 44 —

on the middle Saturday of May. Home advantage proved decisive, Seagry won both the football and netball tournaments.

Opposite page: Top Left: Sarah Appleby, Vanessa Outlaw, Danielle Juson, Leanne Foyle, Natalie Gosling, Claire Gardner and Kimberley Tucker with their winning shield. Bottom left: Natalie Gosling takes a shot; Bottom left: Kimberley Tucker (GD), and Vanessa Outlaw in action; Top right: Hayley Brown.

This page: Top right: Ben Stew, Francis Martin, Mark Lane, Luke Freeth, Lance Heal, James Hatherell, David Rea and Peter Pickard with their winning shield. Above and below: Ben Stew in action. Right and below: Mark Lane with ref Dermo Selwood in the background.

45

This page: As well as teaching children the ways of the world in the classroom, the school also makes sure its youngsters know the ways of the road. Seagry children are luckier than most in that their village is away from main roads - indeed Lower Seagry is one big cul-de-sac - but a bit of cycling proficiency is always valuable, especially with the long summer holidays coming up. Teachers created a course from the school, along the 'main' road and around Broadleaze.

Summer

SUMMERS seem to last longer and be slightly more lazy in West Country villages like Seagry than in the big cities, and when the village primary school sends the children off for the best, hottest and sunniest six weeks from the third week in July, the summer really begins. In the fields, meadows and woods around the village, summer arrives imperceptibly as the lush green of spring is gradually replaced by a hazy, dusty, yellow.

The final summer of the century began with a tease: early June was wet - very wet - but then the end of June and early July saw some very hot days, raising hopes among the frustrated children of a long, hot summer.

But as soon as the school holidays came, the hot weather stuttered somewhat, and a traditional English summer ensued: one hot day, one wet day, followed by three cloudy ones and then a hot day again wiped out with an afternoon thunderstorm. These roll up the Vale, make the electricity pylons crackle even more, literally wring the atmosphere dry, and leave the woods dripping.

Dauntsey Vale summers are always deceptive - you remember the hot days and the memory tricks you into thinking it should be like that from June to the beginning of September.

But 1999's summer was a fair one. Just enough nice days not to make everyone depressed and no parched weeks to worry the farmers.

Most importantly, that great old English optimism which organises a village event on almost every weekend of the summer, despite the probability at least a third of them will be washed out, paid off - the sun smiled on Seagry's summer.

For the first time, new events were added to the usual tea parties, fetes and car boot sales. For the first time, Seagry's magnificent gardens opened their gates, giving villagers the chance to compare and contrast, or simply admire.

AESTHETICALLY, Seagry is reasonably well-endowed with historic and picturesque little cottages, although somehow there isn't the cliched quaintness you'd associate with a near neighbours like famous Castle Combe or Lacock. Seagry would never win the title of 'Prettiest Village', but its villagers are conscientious and proud, and it's won the more coveted Best Kept Village title seven times in 30 years - not bad in a county with more than 200 villages.

The Best Kept competition is hard fought: Seagry came second in its class in 1999, but at least there wasn't the controversy of previous years. One recent year, the village was told it hadn't won because the war memorial was untidy - the village protested it didn't even have a war

Top: Six of the seven Best Kept Village plaques are proudly displayed around the sign for Broadleaze, Seagry's neat estate of 'council' houses. The other one has been lost in the mists of time.

memorial. Still, whether the judges pick Seagry one particular year or not, it will be almost guaranteed every hedge will be trimmed, every verge kept under control and every border edged perfectly. While everyone does their bit, Doug Wiltshire, pictured above with the help of his niece Anne Stent, is the most noticeable Best Keeper of the Best Kept Village.

It's a good job he does - in 1999 Wiltshire County Council decided it could only afford to cut roadside grass twice a year. Doug and Anne are out at least once a week through the summer.

EVERYONE in the village, even the older folk to whom it has been hearth and home for decades, recognises Seagry as a tiny place in a big world. But when the villagers watch the images of war, famine, disease and floods on the news each night, none of them has a direct interest like *Phil Thomas*. For there's a chance this mild mannered Welshman will be watching the news one night, then be flying the plane that's carrying more news cameramen the next.

It happened in 1999 when the year's big conflict in Kosovo kicked off - Phil was there piloting a Hercules and flying the troops, aid and equipment to Skopje and Pristina. This 35-year-old is used to flying sorties in the world's trouble spots. The year also saw him involved in the re-supply of Kuwait - an on-going conflict which isn't, apparently, news anymore - and flights to Bosnia, as well as two major exercises with the USAF in Maryland.

But most of the year was spent training and waiting - a new world emergency means he lives a life on 'standby', three, six or 12 hours away from hopping on board. He joined the RAF at 17 with the dream of being a fighter pilot but 'wasn't good enough' and flew Hercs for ten years before taking up a desk job. But he missed the flying so moved to RAF Lyneham and lived in married quarters at nearby Stanton St Quintin with his wife, Amanda.

He became involved in Seagry life through the cricket club, and opted for a pad of their own just three years ago. From his bedroom window he can't quite see the famous air base which sits on top of the hill a few miles away - he's more pleased it overlooks the cricket pitch. It's a quiet base to return to after trips to all four corners of the world, although Phil is quick to ruefully admit he hasn't quite been all the way round. He's been to the other side - Australia - but came back the same way.

But 1999 won't be a year Phil will remember for his flying achievements - that's just part of the job. This was the year he qualified to represent his country at a sport - to match friend and neighbour Eric Peters. The lad from Cefneithin, Llanelli qualified to represent Wales at fly fishing after a gruelling competition to pick four from 180 of Wales' top fishermen. It was quite an achievement to finish third in the national trials. He was 'very pleased at that'.

TAKING a snapshot of a year in the life of a village is black and white. This is a story of Seagry in the last year of the century. It's a pity though, because for *Jeremy Newman*, the penultimate year of the century was a lot more interesting. So this book can't tell you about his 1998, just his 1999, which was thankfully a lot less eventful.

So we can't explain how he shot to worldwide fame as the manager of Malmesbury's abattoir when two Tamworth boars escaped in January 1998, swam the freezing river and holed up in a copse for a week. How his cheeky grin ended up on TV stations across the world. Nor can we tell you how a freak accident ruled him out of a whole season playing his sporting passion. On the first day of the cricket season in 1998, he slipped on some toys cunningly left at the top of the stairs by young Tom and Daisy Newman, and ended up at the bottom with a fractured and broken ankle. He knew it was the first day of the cricket season - the ambulancemen had to carry him out through the April snow. How his father Tony, a legend in Malmesbury farming circles, suffered and thankfully recovered from a heart attack and how the family business which had served farmers for generations was forced to close as new regulations made it impossible for smaller abattoirs to run at a profit. The site on the edge of Malmesbury was sold for development. No - all those things took place in 1998, but this is a story of 1999 and Jeremy had a quieter year.

After 20 years working at the slaughterhouse, he returned to the family farm in Lea, five miles from his home in Seagry's old schoolhouse which he shares with Tom, Daisy and wife Melanie, to work with 160 beef cattle. From being at the centre of a wide farming community, meeting people everyday, now Jeremy works largely on his own. He celebrated his 37th birthday with a return to his favourite spot - the crease at Malmesbury Cricket Club. He had a good season with the bat, until he pulled a groin muscle at the wicket and had to be carried off by ten other players. "Hopefully, I'll have a full season next year," he says ruefully.

It's fitting we begin a look at the life of Seagry School with a picture of the place many of the children who go to the school first get a taste of learning. These youngsters at Seagry Playgroup, which meets most mornings in the village hall, don't realise it but they're learning complex social and educational processes, just by playing with water and sand, ride-on toys and listening to stories. With a grounding at the playgroup, the move up to 'big' school is child's play.

Seagry Church of England Primary School on the afternoon of May 27, 1999. The smallest ones, th
fairness of that. The adults - here the teachers are joined by everyone involved: the reading helpers, the
Paul took many pictures of this, but not surprisingly, none showed everyone's face clearly and eve
replaced one of those rotating cameras beloved of huge public schools, and that, coupled of course wit

THE BIGGEST day of Seagry School's year probably came on the second Tuesday in February. The school was named as the kind of school other schools should try to emulate. The man making the statement was influential - Chris Woodhead, the government's Chief Inspector of Schools, and when his annual report came out with Seagry's name prominent, the school was swept away for a short while. Newspapers and radio interviews followed, and even The Guardian came to see what made Seagry School so great.

It was something the parents had known for a long time. Here was a small village school with all the community behind it, intimate enough for every child to matter, but not too small to be quaint and isolated.

During the last 20 years of the century, the underlying mood wasn't in favour of small village schools. On cost grounds, which were dubiously backed up with educational reasons, village schools were closed, merged and made bigger. Seagry survived through a process of elimination. Neighbouring villages lost theirs, and Seagry took the school-less children in. Now though, the pendulum has swung back again, and many parents actively seek to send their children to village schools like Seagry. They come from all over to walk up the long drive to the school's front door, and the staff, governors and parents try hard to keep the strong links between the village and the school, even though probably less than half of the children live within

> *"The scho*
> *one other s*
> *to em*
> *something*
> *known f*

*ays get ordered to the front and have to sit on the rock hard school playground - I could never see the
, the secretary and the playground supervisors - get the chairs to sit on, and everyone else has to stand.
at the camera. As with all huge school photographs, this is the best he could do. A wide-angled lens
aved nature of the children, means there's no cheeky kid appearing twice at either end of the back row.

the old parish boundaries.

Amid all the fanfare of being named as a top school, everyone tried and failed, mostly through modesty, to pinpoint the secret behind the school's success. It probably had something to do with the way the school had dealt with the constant changes in educational thinking. Two years of a Labour government meant designated hours for reading, writing and numeracy - but instead of harking back to the ethos held dear in the Victorian school house down the road, the school maintained a relaxed atmosphere and merely adjusted rather than changed all it did before.

But 1999 was a big year for the school, even without the kudos of official recognition. The headteacher for 13 years, James York Moore, taught his last class, held his last staff meeting and, here, with shirt and tie sitting strategically next to the only person in Seagry that day with less hair than he, took part in his last Seagry school photo on a bright, sunny day in June.

After more than a decade he felt the need for a new challenge, and a bigger, busier school on the other side of the clay vale at Cherhill beckoned.

In Mr York Moore's penultimate month in charge, disaster almost struck. June's heavy rain blocked the drainpipes and the school's many flat roofs became flooded. The quick thinking of neighbour and unassuming voluntary school handyman, Dermo Selwood, who clambered up in the rain to unblock and clear, saved the day.

Everyone helps out at the school, especially with reading. But whereas the children of the past might have read in a big group, now they read to themselves, to each other and to the dedicated band of parents and former parents who just come in for the joy of hearing children read aloud.

But like most schools, Seagry doesn't look back, except in history lessons. Every child has access to and lessons on computers in the school - even though they live in a rural, farming community, Seagry school children will leave very much part of the 21st century's computer age.

Top right: Reading time for Polly Bell and Edward Martin; Above: Infants Jake Warr and Ann Webb read with former dinner lady of 31 years Margaret Collins; Right: Samantha Drummond and Kelly Hibberd on the computer; Below: Maths in pairs - Jesse Nash and Edward King.

Facing page.
Top left: Danielle Juson with headteacher James York Moore.
Top Right: Reece Clark on the computer with teacher Tracy Cornelius.
Middle right: Natasha Teixeira buried in a book.
Bottom right: School governor Audrey Barnes helps out with reading too, this time with Kristina Appleby and Max Clilverd, while Max's brother Jamie reads on his own (bottom left).
Inset: Zoe Bailey deep in thought.

55

Left: Quiet concentration is easy to find at the school, even with a sunny summer day outside. Senior class pupils Tom Carndo and Alex James complete their comprehension lesson.

Left: Ben Parfitt in deep thought as he gets to grips with his English lesson.

The hushed anticipation of the dinner queue, *below*. The children patiently waiting behind the lucky first in line couldn't really line up much closer together so the meals must be pretty good.

Along with the moves to close many smaller village primary schools, Seagry also resisted the widespread closure of many small school kitchens.

While lots of schools now have their hot dinners brought by a touring van, Seagry School still has traditional dinner ladies, like Irene Lewis *(behind the counter, below right)* who cook, serve, supervise and naturally end up as the next best thing to mums for the younger ones.

A neighbour of Irene's on Broadleaze, Suzanne Tucker, has the most popular job - handing out puddings *(above)*.

Not all Seagry youngsters have school dinners: young Joseph Kidner's packed lunch *(previous page, inset)* brings a little bit of home comfort to school.

Above: Seagry is one of just two state-funded primary schools in the county with its own swimming pool. The round pool takes a great deal of managing, but comes into its own in the summer, as Class Three show. For 22 years Joy Selwood took time out every day to maintain the pool, and handed the job over, complete with new pool liner, to Chris Shipp in June.

Below: Headteacher James York Moore (left) and governor Audrey Barnes keep an eye on things at playtime. Left: Forget computer games, Pokemon and bullying, traditional pleasures of the playground don't change, as Samantha Drummond and Kelly Hibberd show.

THERE was a touch of deja vu for housewife, mum and general doer *Clare Clilverd* in the early part of 1999. Sitting in the pub, word went round that the village hall committee needed a chairman. Everyone said Clare would do it, and she found herself with the role, when all she went into the pub for was a quiet drink.

It wasn't a surprise. Within months of moving to the village, Clare's twin sons Max and Jamie (eldest son Fraser is three years the senior) joined the village playgroup - Clare was the new chairman of the playgroup for two years. When the boys went to the village primary school, Clare was the chair of the Friends of Seagry School - a position she held until February.

With husband Rob running his own advertising business in Bristol and the Bristol Colts rugby team, and the boys sport mad, Clare says she has a lot of time for involvement in the life of the village - time for things like the Open Garden Day, which took place in the summer. "I think it was the first time anyone had ever tried anything like that in Seagry," she said. "It was something that James York Moore wanted to do because there were so many nice gardens in the village and one day he realised he'd never really walked around the village - despite being the school headteacher for so many years.

"And with many of the children not coming from Seagry itself, we thought it would be a nice idea to encourage parents to get to know the village too."

After getting permission from the owners, a tour was devised to take place on the day of the school fete, starting at the school itself, and ending with cream teas in the courtyard in the middle of the Clilverd's home. It was just the sort of thing Clare loves - villagers out and about, meeting each other and having a laugh. "I like living in the village - there's such a lovely sense of community."

HER official title is school administration officer, but *Debbie Short* is much more than that. A shoulder to cry on for the youngsters, and increasingly for the bureaucracy-laden staff too, dinner money keeper, first aider, go-between, organiser and general dogsbody, the days when the school secretary kept a note of children present and the doings of the day on one page of a log book are long gone. So it's probably just as well that Debbie lists her hobbies as her family.

She has four who've suddenly grown up and are out in the world doing things like flying planes, studying, nursing and caring, while back at home, mum gets on with running the village primary school. She was playgroup leader for five years before the lure of a part-time job making sure the school ran smoothly was up for grabs 11 years ago. Since then, the job has changed 'out of all proportion' as the hours a week the school demands has risen from 15 to nearer 30. "The technology has taken over. Now it's as much about managing your cheque book as it is keeping record books. I do have helplines to call and other administrators at other schools, so we support each other."

"You have to be a Jack of all trades: Everything from sorting out a child's dinner money to the overall finance of the school. A lot of work is liaison with parents and governors, and making sure the admin side of the school runs as smoothly as possible."

Amazingly, she still has time to help out elsewhere in the school. She helps run a netball club and even a mum's netball team.

Originally from Sussex, Debbie married a man from Chippenham (Maurice - who has worked at engineering firm Westinghouse for 40 years) and moved to Seagry from Cheltenham in 1970. The idyllic scene of a country cottage in a peaceful village with roses over the door and a stream in the back garden was their dream, and they largely achieved that, although the stream in the back garden is probably more like a ditch.

They chose Lower Seagry, set up home, extended it twice and now, even though the birds have flown the nest, Debbie doesn't think she will move.

"In Lower Seagry there hasn't been that much change. One or two spaces have been 'infilled', and obviously the people are different but it is still very quiet and like it used to be. Perhaps you could call it a timewarp."

Just a stone's throw from the children and their text books are the woods that shelter the village from western approaches. Deer have probably lived there for centuries, if not millennia. Now no one, from kings to farm hands, bothers them with either shotgun or hounds - only very occasionally is the odd one shot to keep a tab on numbers.

Captured in a shaft of early morning sun, these two *(above)* heard the camera shutter and were soon off into the shadows.

Their inate wariness towards Seagry's human inhabitants means not many villagers can catch more than a glimpse of these beautiful creatures, save for a sight everyone in Seagry dreads, a deer startled in the glare of car headlights.

Deer roam pretty freely on the farmland around the village - and don't just stick to the secret woods on the higher ground. A fair-sized herd live down by the river on Trinity Farm.

Opposite page: Unless they've been sneaking around the village in the dead of night, this is the view of Upper Seagry the deer get to see. Looking east from the woods, the Stanton road that leads to The New Inn and The Knoll is behind the hedge coming in from the right. The main house in the centre is Chestnut Lodge.

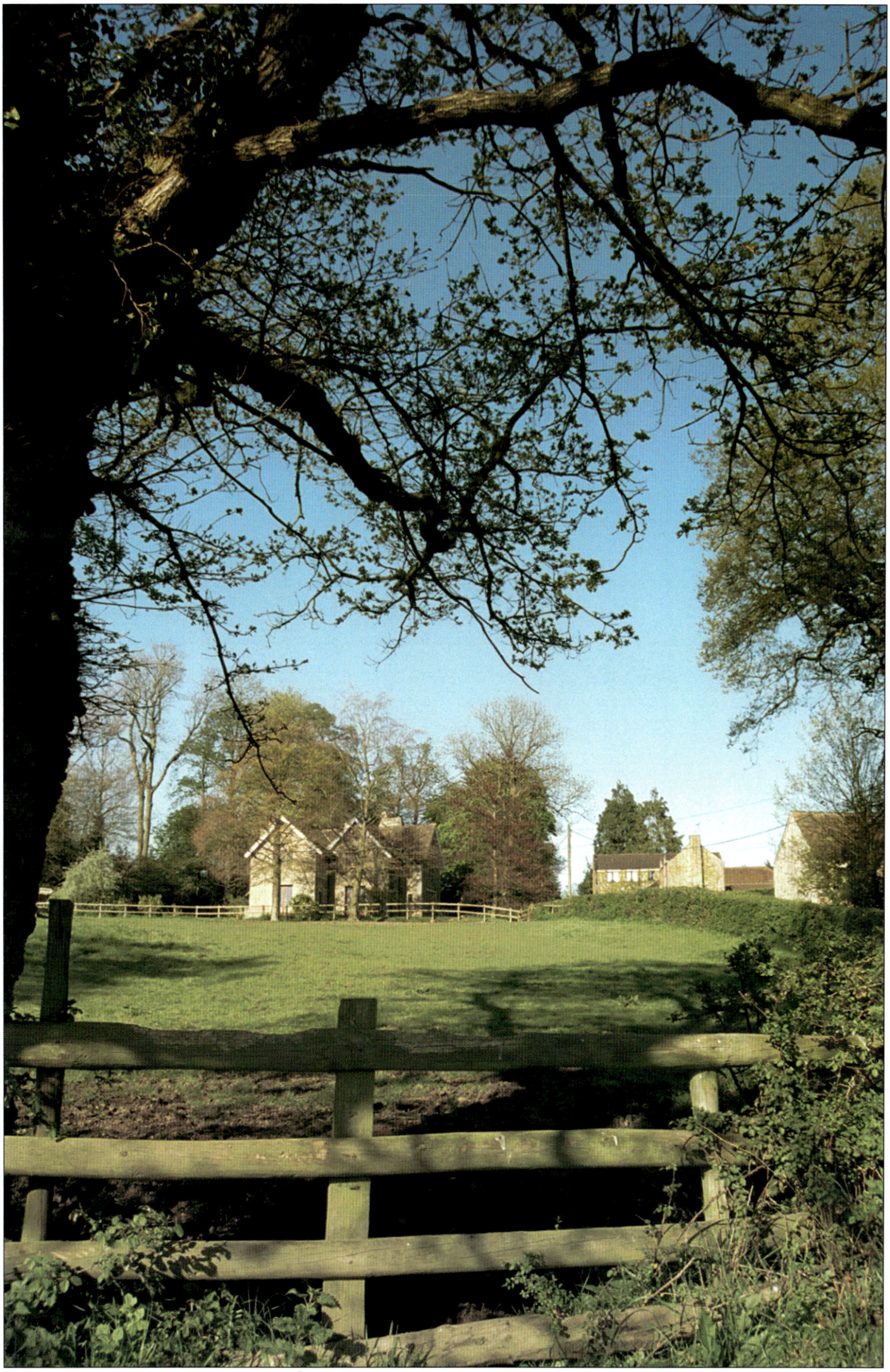

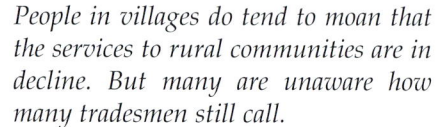

People in villages do tend to moan that the services to rural communities are in decline. But many are unaware how many tradesmen still call.

The postman (top), the council dustmen (left), the mobile library (below), the mobile fish 'n' chip shop (above, right), the coal man (right) and the daily bus service - not to mention the mobile shop that is said to come fortnightly, but managed to evade the lens.

No need to cook the dinner on a Wednesday night in Seagry - it's brought to your door with a smile. At eight o'clock sharp the mobile fish 'n' chip van pulls up in Broadleaze.

Left: One for the mums of 2010 to embarrass the teenagers with when the first girl/boyfriend visits. Taken at the dress rehearsal on midsummer's day, the ensuing week saw Seagry School's annual production: 'The Land Of Make Believe' with sketches from Peter Pan, Alice In Wonderland, Cinderella, The Pied Piper, Pinocchio, Dumbo and Snow White.

Right: To mark the Millennium, few schools would have had a seaside garden built. The nearest proper seaside is 40 miles away so the children loved school governor and Mr Fix-it Dermo Selwood's creation. The boat was donated by Chippenham's Sea Cadets and fits 15 on board at a push. It was James York Moore's idea for a designated garden area, and ten turned out on the first Saturday morning of work. Numbers dwindled, and just Dermo finished the job.

THE VAGARIES of the English summer in two easy examples. Soggy grass, muddy tyres, waterproof coats and a brolly are *de rigueur* for the villagers and parents attending the Friends of Seagry School Car Boot Sale on the second Saturday of June *(opposite page, bottom)*.

The grey skies did more threatening than actual raining, but the bargain hunters turned out for a great fund-raising event, which included a white elephant stall and a raffle. Organisers were optimistic though, and arranged an ice cream stall.

Everyone knows the irony that car boot sales don't sell car boots, but Seagry's did. One chap came all the way from Swindon to sell not just his car boot but his entire car.

Another day, another event, another season. Just four weeks later and the annual school fete was bathed in sunshine, smattered with shorts and tasteful shirts.

Everyone mucks in for a bit of fun, manning stalls and attractions. This year's had quad biking *(above)*, pony rides, skittles, a toddlers' corner, tombola, cake stall, lucky dip and a greasy pole.

Wellie-wanging is a must for any self-respecting fete - Jim Stent tries his luck *(below left)*, while Rob Clilverd gives a helping hand to Callum Harford on the mini golf *(right)*.

If all that excitement wasn't enough, an early evening family barbecue was followed by a children's disco and everyone thanked the weather for a great day.

THE WORLD became a slightly smaller place during 1999 - and the concept of a global village reached the relatively quiet backwaters of Seagry during the year.

Born and bred in the village, *Jessica Mills* celebrated her 21st birthday in a year which also took her to Bulgaria to undertake voluntary work for the United Nations. For a fortnight in August, she was one of 10 multinational volunteers running a summer camp for more than 100 teenagers at an orphanage in the Bulgarian city of Plovdiv. Jessica graduated from the University of Wales at Swansea during 1999 with a high 2:1 in development studies, before returning to begin an MA in social development.

In Bulgaria, Jessica's main tasks were to organise activities for the children, aged between 14 and 19, but given the run-down nature of the facilities, her team of 'Westerners' were also persuaded to do maintenance work including painting and fixing things. "The conditions were fairly dire and the food was appalling. There was no lighting, no hot water and lots of things needed doing. We mainly organised sports activities but they were teenagers so within half an hour of doing something, they would be bored and want to do something else." The language barrier was less of a problem than she imagined. "I have no Bulgarian, they spoke some English, but there were ten different languages in our group alone, so we tended to use a lot of sign language." Jessica returned to Seagry for the last time in the 20th century to be with her family at Christmas. "It changes every time I go away and come back again. I went to Seagry Primary School which was great because there was a big group of us in the village the same age. It did become a bit less exciting but I still really liked it, even when I was a teenager. Now when I come back, the village is full of so many people I don't know. It's grown a lot but I like village life and the whole community spirit. I hate big cities and hope I don't live in one when I eventually leave home. I'd like to stay in Seagry but I don't think it would help me to do what I want to do, which is working for an international charity."

It wasn't just a momentous year for Jessica, in 1999. Her younger sister Gemma, a pupil at Hardenhuish School in Chippenham, passed her GCSEs with five A* and four A grades, while father John trekked through the Alps. The family, which also include Jessica's mum Jennifer and brother Barnaby, have lived in Seagry for more than two decades.

A QUINTESSENTIAL English garden, right in the heart of the village. Only *Agnes Riley's* gloriously colourful corner of Seagry takes on added significance considering the last few weeks of the year saw her celebrate her 79th birthday. With her sight failing and the body not quite as able as it used to be, Agnes' garden is a wonder of the village and both are pictured here on the day it formed part of the first gardens 'open day' in Seagry.

The secret to her success is a simple one: The idea, she says, is to plant so many flowers that the weeds don't have any room to grow. But this modesty belies the wisdom gained from years of nurturing, pruning and caring for plants. Despite losing her husband Charles nine years ago - he did the heavy work - Agnes continues to produce a sparkling garden every year. She will always call it 'his' garden, although nowadays, grandson Richard comes over to do the mowing. This summer was the 43rd that Agnes had planted and nurtured in Seagry. She arrived in the days when the village had shops and businesses. Now, she quickly calls it a 'dead' village, with just a pub, post box, phone box and school. Village life has dropped off terribly, she says, and now all her neighbours go to work in places like Chippenham every day. "There's nobody around any more. People keep telling me to get an emergency alarm, and I think 'gosh, that's what it's coming to...'"

After giving up driving in 1997, she doesn't get out too much, although the village hall provides an occasional place to meet up with old friends and enjoy lunches and beetle drives. The problem is that not a lot of young people can afford to stay here, she says. The continuity has gone, and there are few left in the village who, like her, have lived in Seagry all their lives.

Another school year comes to a close *(top)* with 1999 being a special year not only for the eldest pupils but also for James York Moore who departed as head teacher. Also to leave was Tracy Cornelius. A joint presentation evening was held on July 21 *(right)* and Mr York Moore's biggest of many presents was a garden shredder *(below left)*. Mr York Moore is now the headteacher of Cherhill School, the 11-year-olds now catch the bus to secondary schools in Chippenham (below) or Malmesbury, but Miss Cornelius is a bit further afield - at St Christopher's School, Penang, Malaysia.

67

Seagry in summer means one thing for most villagers - gardening.

These next pages (66-79 inclusive) are devoted to a selections of gardens and houses within the village. The first seven show the gardens that took part in Seagry's Garden Route which were open to the public during the summer to complement the school's summer fete.

Then the variety of different sizes and styles of Seagry's houses are featured, from Jacobean through Regency and Victorian with Cotswold cottages right up to the modern day.

Many of the descriptions of the gardens formed the trail guide, devised by Clare Clilverd to accompany the event, or have been penned by the gardeners themselves.

Centred in the middle of the village is a row of cottages which are also a picture. This particular garden largely comprises of an immaculate lawn which is surrounded by flower beds. In the summer it is mainly planted with dahlias, grown from seed. Other favourites include fuchsias and sweet peas. The cottage garden was awarded a 'Highly Commended' by the North Wiltshire District Council for their entry in the 'Best Florally Decorated Front Garden' category in the North Wiltshire Flower Festival, during the final year of the century. The garden which contains a variety of colour also features an ornamental pond which was installed two years previously and is currently stocked with goldfish and koi carp.

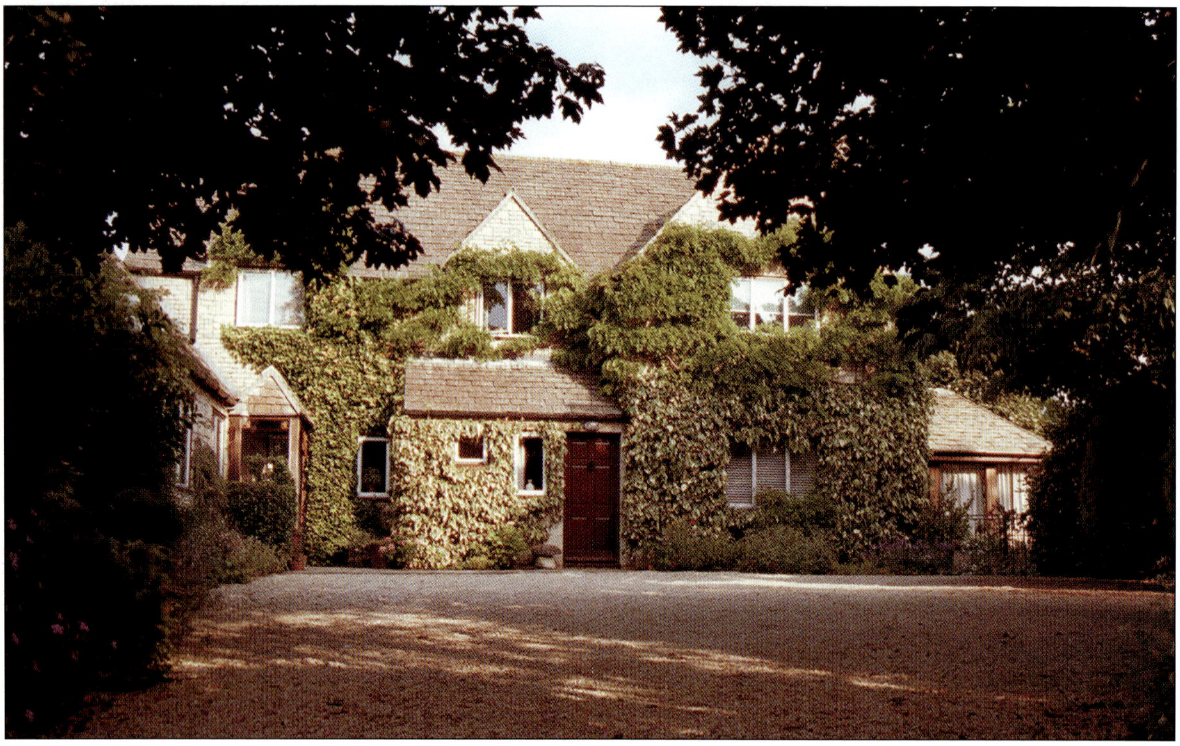

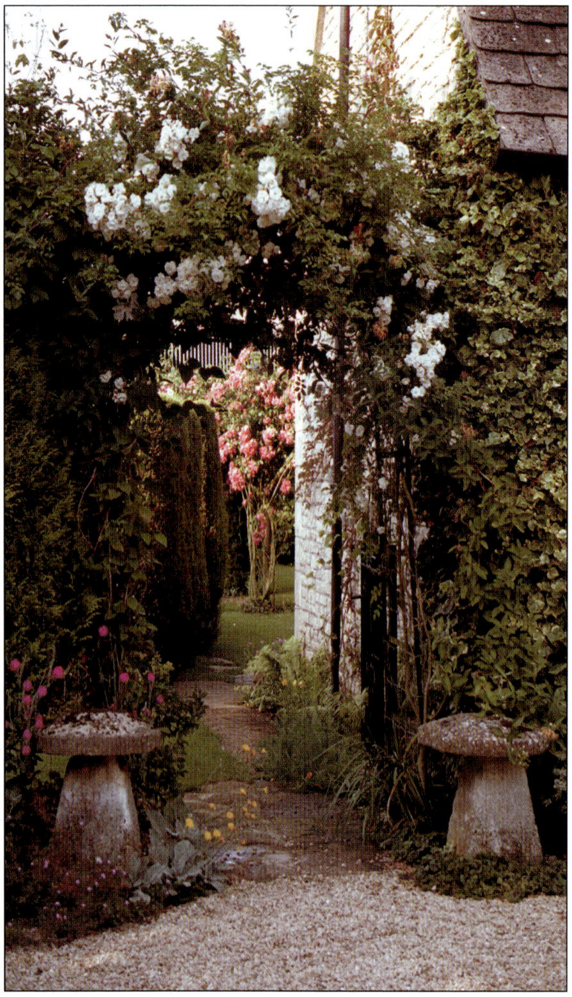

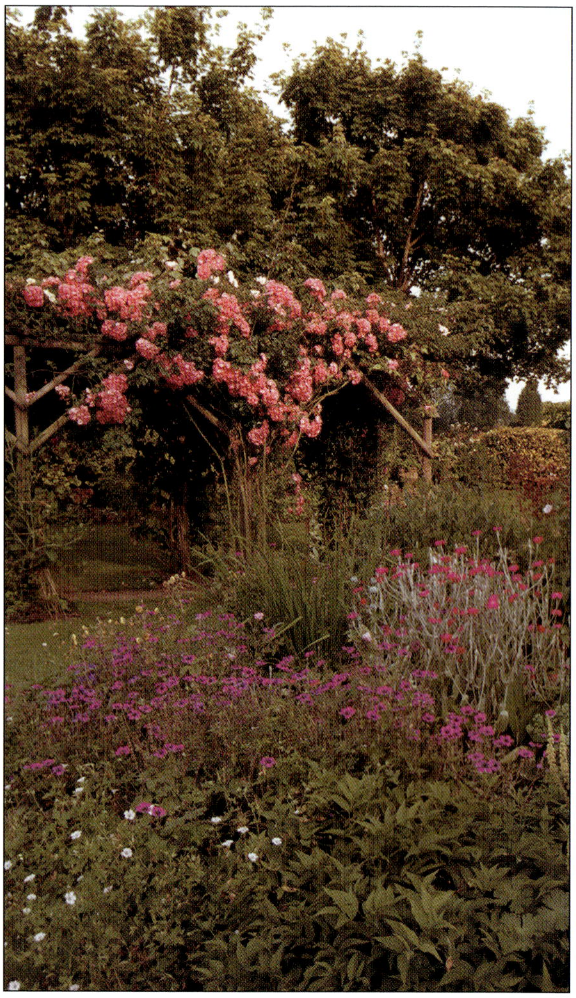

Views of the garden at Sturmage House *(left)*. The house, built in 1980, appears to be much older and the breathtaking garden adds to the feeling of age.

The stunning garden has wonderful herbaceous borders and a different variety of trees. Real herbaceous and perennial plants with hardy geraniums can be found. This is a garden where existing plants are divided up and shared amongst other neighbouring gardens.

The Chestnuts *(this page)* lies in the middle of the village. A 'William and Mary' house built around 1700, it is Grade II-listed and its gardens stand in about a three-quarters of an acre with far reaching views across the Dauntsey Vale to the Cherhill Monument.

In front of the house, the garden contains two long borders which are filled with shrubs and ground-cover plants such as spiraea, abelia grandiflora and photina red robin, to provide colour throughout the year. The grounds contain three large grassed areas, where croquet is sometimes played: The perfect setting for those lazy hazy summer months.

IN Agnes Riley's garden, 1999 will go down as the year of the slug. They were so vibrant: tiny little slugs so small they could hardly be seen. She often got up in the morning to find the stem of a flower remaining and all the flowers and leaves completely gone. She had never known it so bad.

The garden *(right)* gained honours in local competitions a few years back, although Agnes is dismissive of some of her competitors who, rather than planting seeds and helping them grow into flowers, preferred things called garden 'centres' and bought plants to put in the garden. She doesn't call that gardening.

Apart from the abundance of roses, the traditional English flower, delphiniums, pansies and lupins made an appearance, with petunias giving depth to the display.

Unlike some gardeners, she is open about her little corner of colour. "I don't mind people coming to have a look. The open day was a nice idea, so people could see different gardens. It brought people into the village and got people chatting. I don't think anyone came in to my garden as such, you can see it all if you lean over the wall."

The water feature of Magpie's Patch, sits in the grounds of a one time two-up-two-down, now a spacious family home. The garden has taken many forms in the past 12 years with the present owners who describe themselves as 'amateurs!'

"Its one thing to enjoy gardening, but it's quite a different matter knowing what you are doing", Anthea Lanning - daughter of a former professional gardener.

This beautiful cottage, known as Dove Cottage, was built in around 1790: The present owners of the cottage found a ha'penny under the flagstones dating back to this era. This was originally the schoolhouse and local children were not only taught the three R's by the lady of the cottage, but also, more importantly how to make bagging hooks - for this they were given the grand sum of one penny a week. The garden displays a wealth of colour in June, from senecio and elaeagnus in the background to the blue of delphiniums, the yellow of lysimachia, the pink of penstemons and many others in the foreground.

A variety of summer bedding plants is interwoven with alchemilla, ajuga and anchusa to provide a kaleidoscope of colour along the borders.

A one-time builder's yard and a chicken run, the garden of Longtyme, near the school grounds (right) has been transformed over the years. Described by the owners as a garden to include as many features as possible on a small scale, it includes a heather bed, blue and pink hyacinths and plant pots in the summer using fuchsia, geraniums, petunias and lobelia.

Pictured on both pages: Manor Farm was built in the early part of the 18th century, with an impressive aspect from both the front (above) and the back (below right). This Queen Anne style with double gable house is also the home for a large 'family': 634 doves to be precise. The dovecote to the south east of the house is itself a listed building.

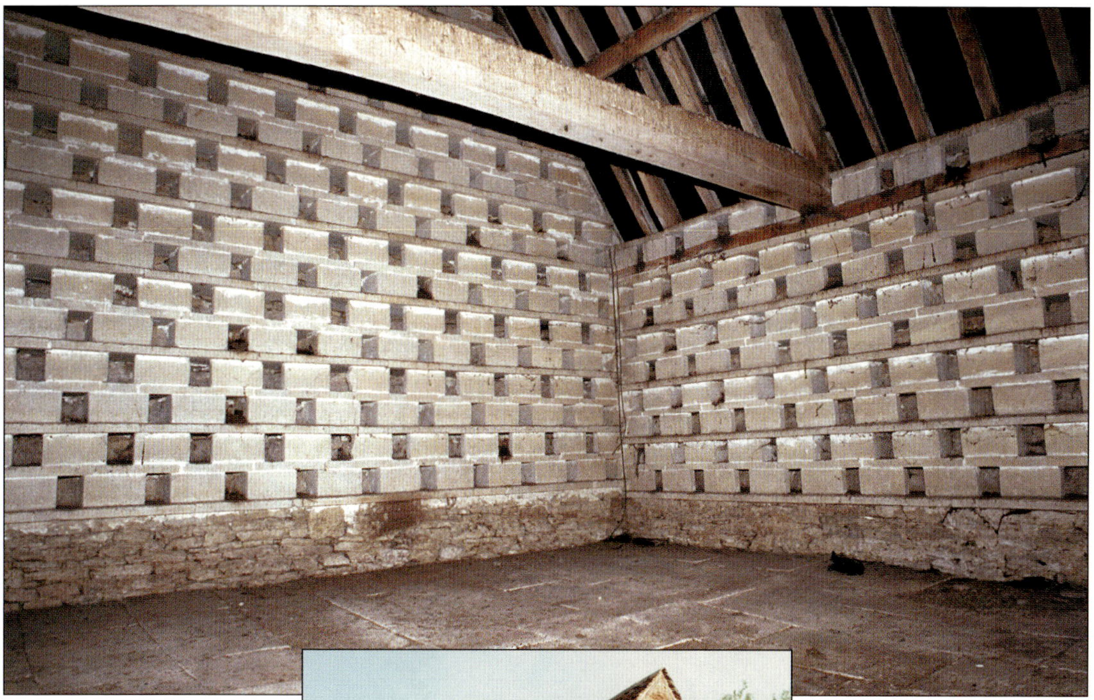

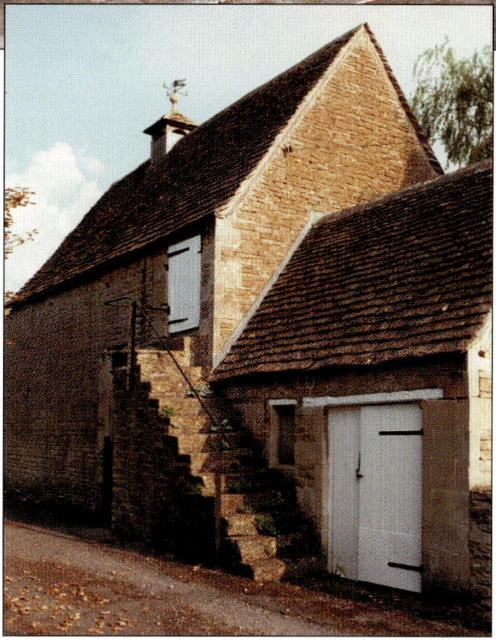

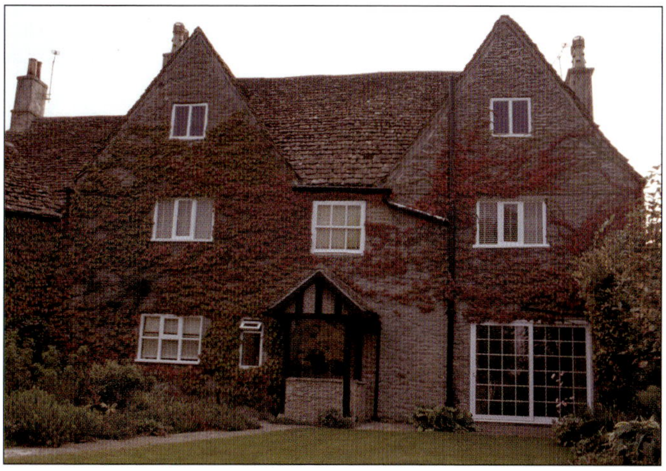

Surrounded in four acres, Seagry House stands near the cricket field and is approached by an avenue of trees *(page 103)* and listed gates. The main feature of the garden has always been the furlong of yew hedging, divided into four sections, creating a wonderful backdrop for delphiniums, agapanthus and euphorbia. The gardens also contain twelve dry ponds in the ornamental water garden and a Ha Ha with blue flowers to give the effect of water. The swimming pool beside the house *(above)* is reputed to be one of the oldest in the county and always brings delight to the village children who are allowed to use it during the summer months. *(Right): The summer house in the grounds and (below) The Lodge.*

Seales Court is an imposing property to the south of Upper Seagry, at the motorway end of the village. Rumour, turned to myth over the years since, has it that when Princess Anne married local boy Captain Mark Phillips in 1973, they looked seriously at Seales Court to set up home. His family home was up the road at Great Somerford, so it would have been convenient. But legend also has it that the security guys had a look and didn't like the proximity of the motorway, so they chose Gatcombe Park a few miles away instead.

The superb gardens were laid out by Percy Cane, and the house itself is shielded well by trees during the summer months.

Seagry End (above) isn't, in fact, at the end of Lower Seagry's cul-de-sac, Trinity Farm is further on. One of many homes nearby to have been lovingly restored.

Pear Tree House (left) stands in the former gardens of Pear Tree Cottage and is part of the limited growth of Seagry towards the end of the Millennium, when new houses were only permitted within the existing village boundaries. The house was designed to reflect the traditional gables and tiled roof of the house opposite - Manor Farm.

It was completed in January making it the last house to be built in the village in the 20th century.

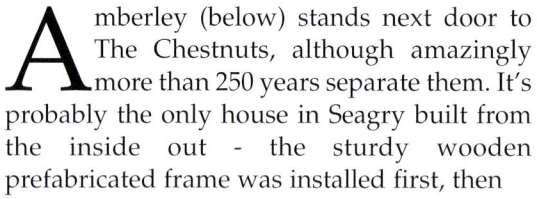

Amberley (below) stands next door to The Chestnuts, although amazingly more than 250 years separate them. It's probably the only house in Seagry built from the inside out - the sturdy wooden prefabricated frame was installed first, then

Above: Two more pretty homes. Rookery Bungalow (left), in between Upper and Lower Seagry, and Windsmeet, (right) near the school.

the red bricks were added around the outside as a reverential nod to next door.

A view of the New Inn at Seagry (above) taken from the side looking towards the Little Knoll in summer.

Church Farm at Lower Seagry (right) is a farmhouse with no farmer. Much of the land was sold to neighbouring farmers, and now horses are the only animals to remain. Unlike many of fine large houses with gates to mark the entrance, this particular house is marked with an ancient Tithe Barn (below) which was once used to collect the tithes of the parish.

Known by the photographer as *Amanda's Garden* - this particular garden in the Courtyard was first created in 1997 after the builders finished converting Seagry House's stables into smart homes. With just grass and a hornbeam hedge as a boundary the secret garden (left) has been magically transformed after many visits to the garden centre and 'borrowing' cuttings and plants from gardening friends. The garden is at its best in July but is designed to be planted for year round interest.

In 1999 a seating area was created in the north-eastern corner of the garden - a hot spot which catches the warm sun all day. The owners say there's nothing nicer than to sit listening to the small water feature while planning the garden's future in the new Millennium. Some of the plants featured are: lavender, heuchera with its lovely red leaves, the bright yellow of rudbeckia and the hebes that flower right through to the autumn.

Another garden in the Courtyard, this too was created from scratch. The lawn was eliminated for ease of maintenance. The main theme of the garden was to create colour all year round, which proved quite a challenge from a shaded garden. However the garden colours at its best in the month of June.

After three years the garden was structurally completed by its owners during 1999 (right). Within the design are three levels of raised beds with the feature being the central pond. In addition, there is a small hexagonal cedar summerhouse and a heated greenhouse in which orchids are grown.

The Courtyard's communal flower bed. This colourful bed was created in 1999, planted with the annuals antirrhinum and petunia with more permanent evergreens broom, variegated hollies, dogwood and euonymus.

When the gardening's done, the New Inn Shooting Club return to their pleasures. The clay pigeons still get blown to bits, the faces are still the same, but now the shooters can leave their coats at home and some even risk shorts. Shooting in the summer is always a bit more pleasurable, the trigger fingers aren't quite so cold.

The weir down at Seagry Mill wasn't always so industrial-looking, and with one of the many electricity pylons that run along the Dauntsey Vale in the background, this could almost be a bit of wasteground on one of Birmingham's canals. But appearances deceive and the River Avon at Seagry's lowest point is a tranquil, picturesque spot, where the hurly-burly of life is a long way away. You can almost feel the sun beating down, the heat coming off the riverside flora and the spellbinding hum that comes with a hot afternoon down by the river. Man has probably taken fish from the fertile waters of the Avon for millennia, but now it's done for pleasure rather than necessity. The only necessity here is a good sun hat, good bait and a net with no holes in.

SUMMER draws on, and the fruits of the warm sun need bringing in from the fields.
Seagry contains all types of farming, large and small, cows to corn. While the fields may be plentiful around the village, most farmers find it economical to hire in agricultural contractors to harvest the yearly crop.

WILL it rain, or won't it? The question most villagers ask themselves each summer morning can't be answered by the Jersey herd *(above)* at Hardinge Farm, tucked between the western woods, the village and the motorway. It could be an advert for butter, though.
The final year saw a strange middle ground. Farmers who'd abandoned beef after the recent BSE crisis now abandoned dairy because of plummeting milk prices. These Charolais cattle *(below)* find a bit of peace on Nables Farm.

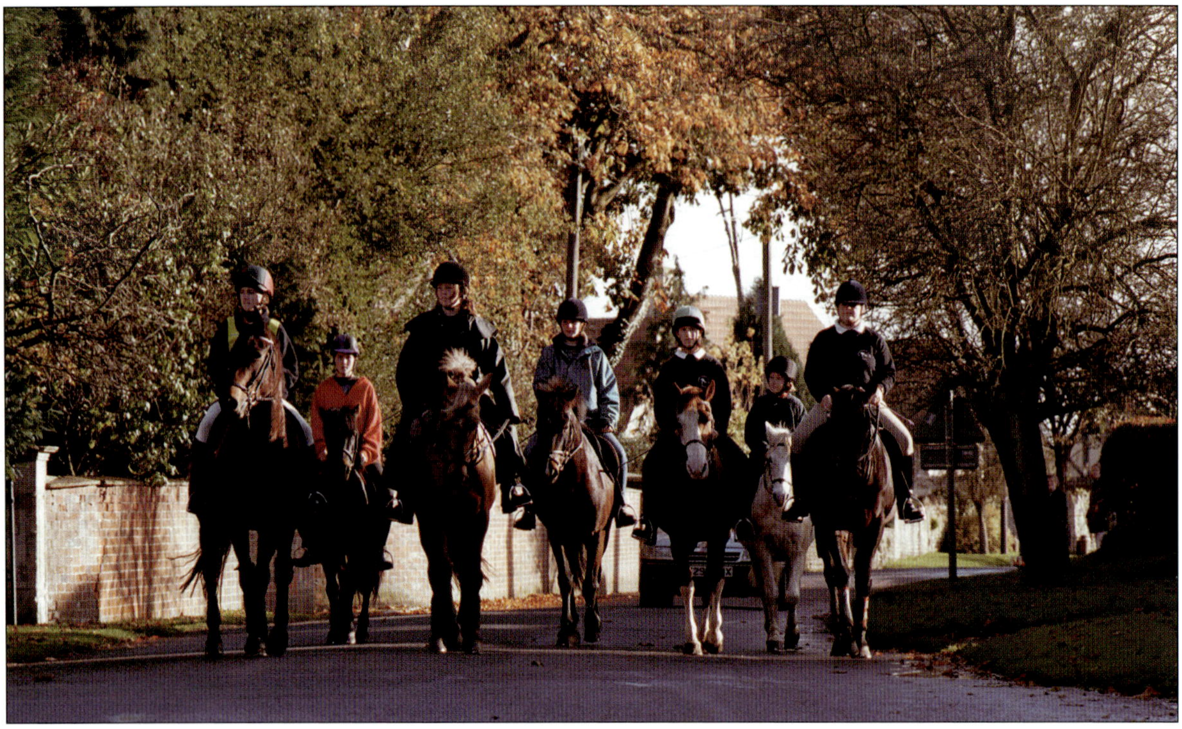

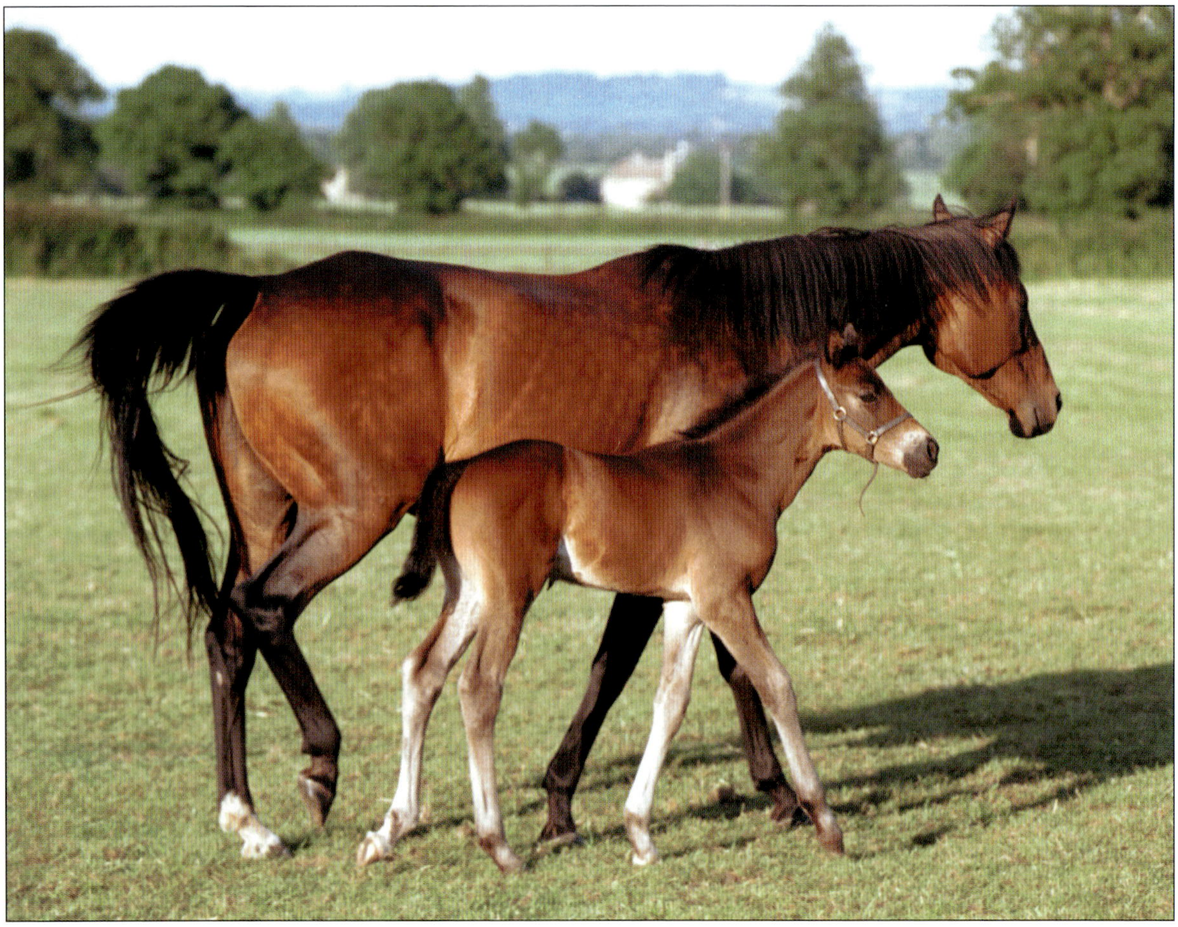

On most summer days, not much moves in Seagry apart from the horse. Seagry is renowned for its stables and the country lanes, farmyards, woods and fields are almost perfect for equine pursuits.

Even if you don't own a horse, there are several stables including The Rookery, between Upper and Lower Seagry, and at Church Farm in Lower Seagry where villagers can hire and ride. Sophie Lanning's family removals firm allows her to indulge: The 15-year-old *(right)* tries to get out and ride her Arab thoroughbred gelding, aptly called Moving Experience, every day after school.

"I think a lot of people have horses and a lot come to ride here because we've got the woods, and there's lots of fields we can play in," said Sophie.

Farmers are particularly horse-friendly in the village. One of Rob Dickinson's horses had a foal this year *(below left)*, and the Beaufort Hunt visits annually at a variety of farmyard locations.

But to paint an idyllic picture of a village where the horse is still king, or the main mode of transport, would be misleading.

The 'progress' towards the new Millennium brings increasing danger for riders. The sign *(below)* spells out the message to drivers, but too many speed round those N-bends, and confrontations are inevitable. Luckily, there's only been one serious accident recently. Two of the Biggin girls from Trinity Farm were caught on horseback near the bridge over the motorway, and one was knocked unconscious in the smash, which also killed her horse. Both have given up riding since.

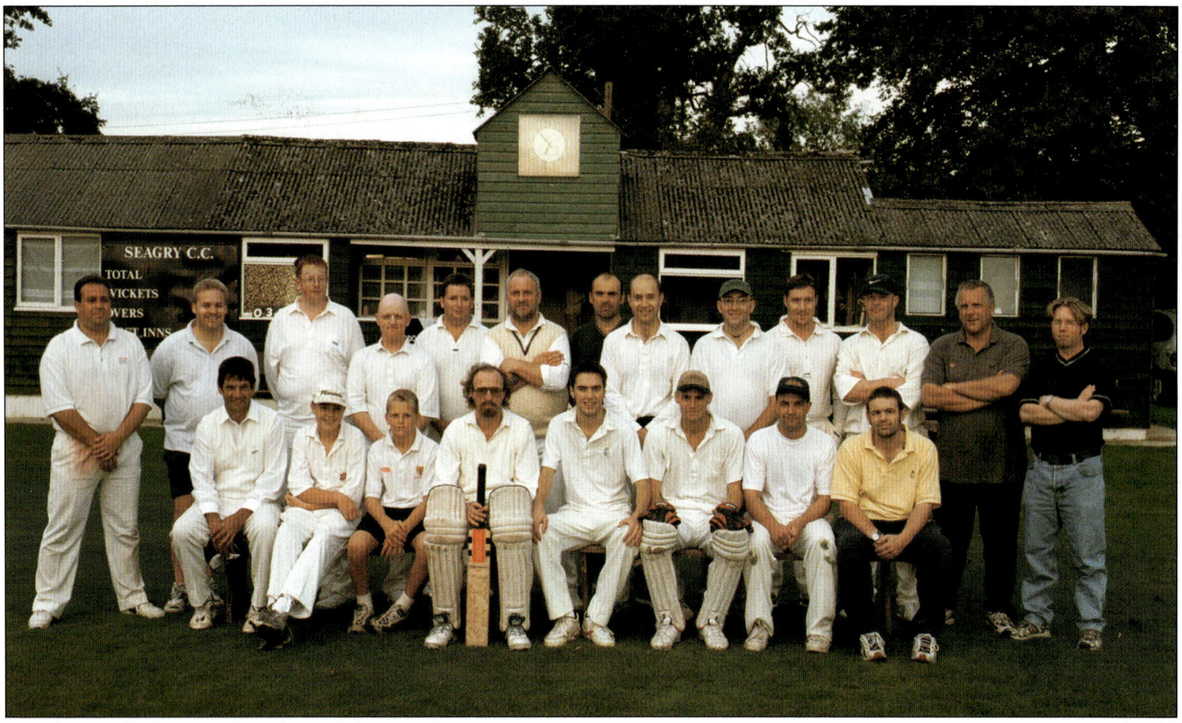
SEAGRY C.C.
TOTAL

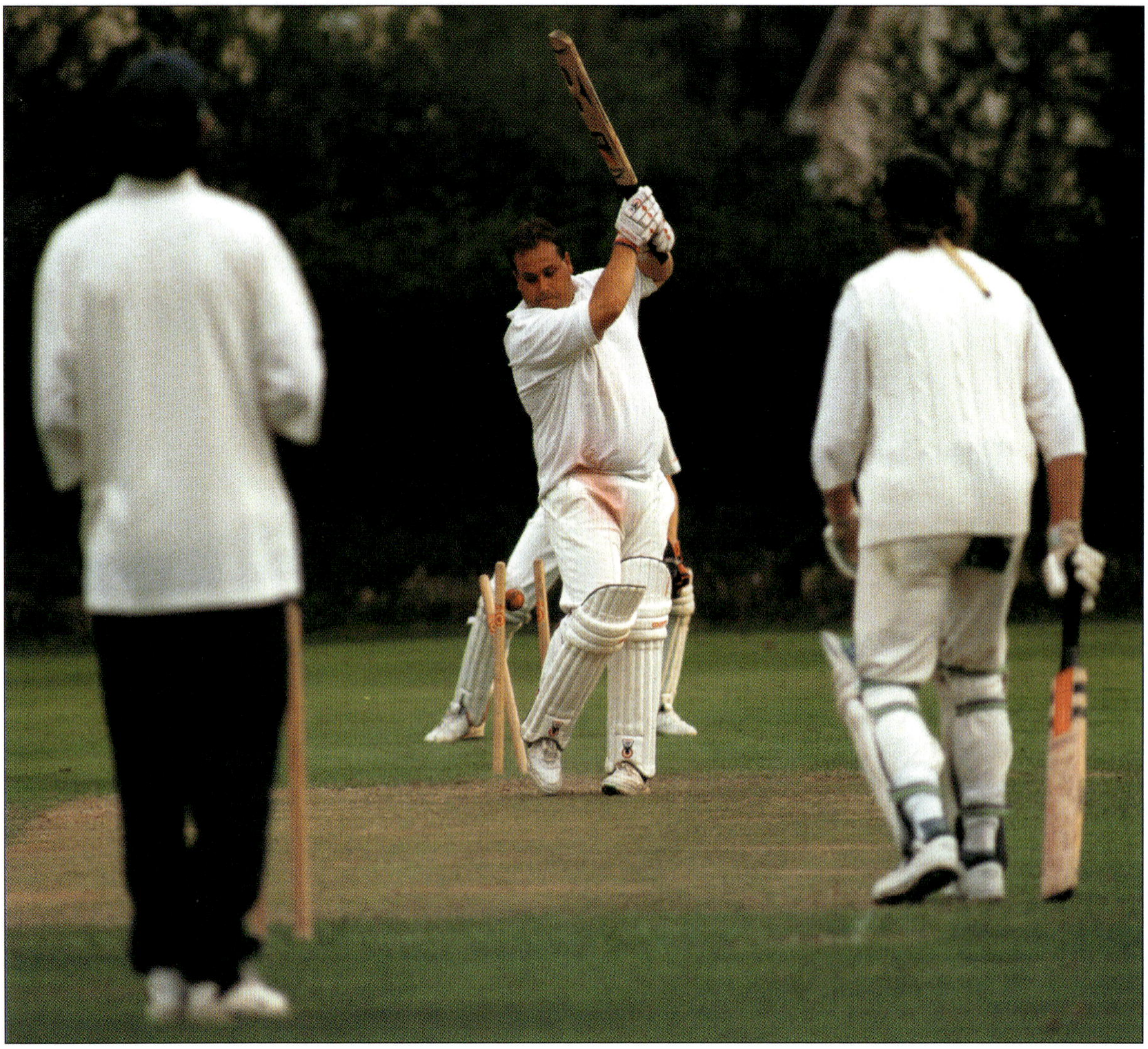

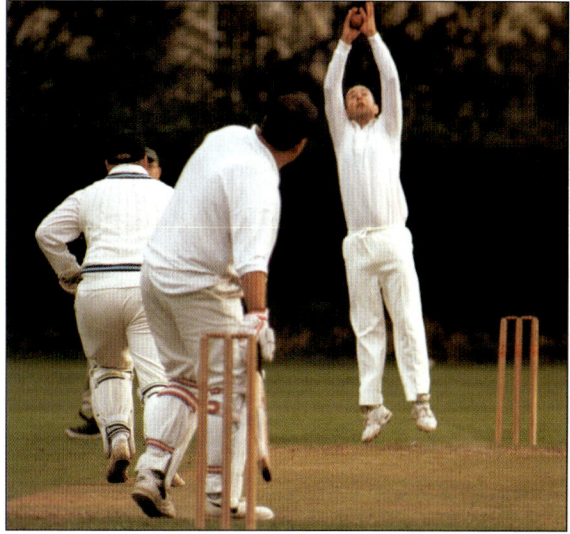

Keep your head straight, follow the bowler's arm and keep a straight bat in line with the ball. The classic forward defence, as displayed by Seagry's cricketers. But it looks like a good day for the bowlers, or is it just that every time Paul aimed his camera, the thought of being captured in action at the crease made the batsmen play crazy, kamikaze shots which ended up with them losing their wickets?

Still, Seagry was always going to be the real winner of this match, captured at the end of the season on the picturesque ground at the front of Seagry House. For the teams were made up of regulars and occasionals from Seagry's club in an end-of-term celebration. The cricketers set aside the serious business of league matches in a game they couldn't lose - judging by the batting displays here, though, it was probably just as well.

Among those who succumbed was captain and former Seagry resident Paul Lewis, who still keeps links with the village through the club. He's the one on the bottom left, showing that if you make an angle like that with your legs, your stumps will end up the same way. Still, the red marks on his trousers show he's really a bowler.

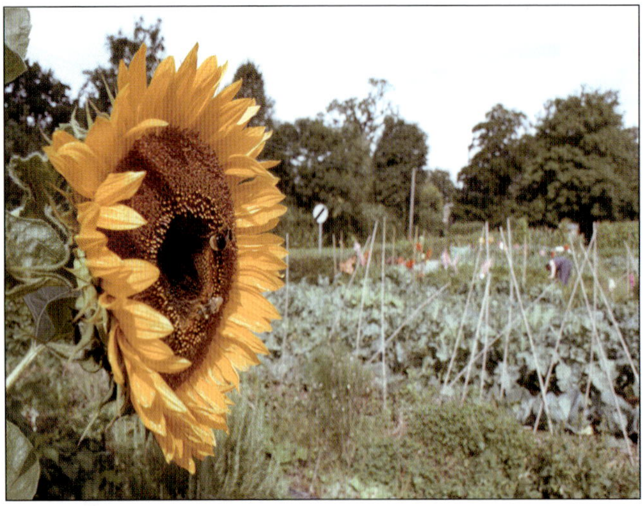

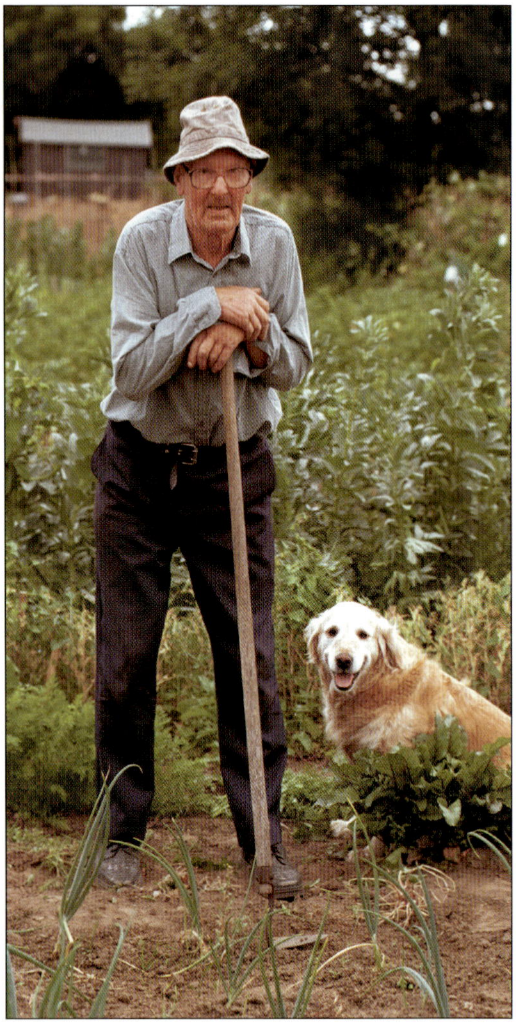

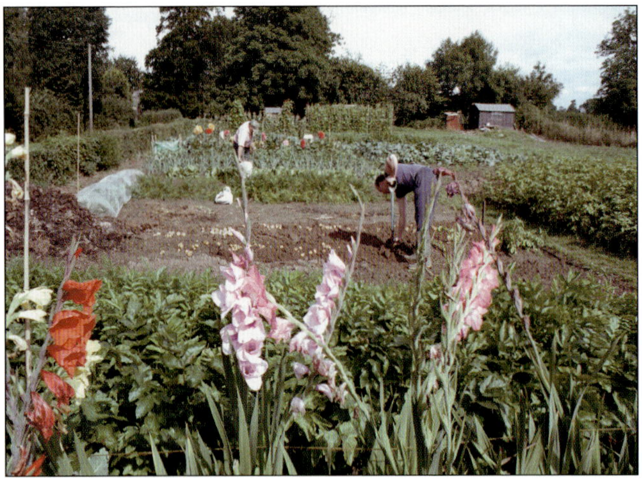

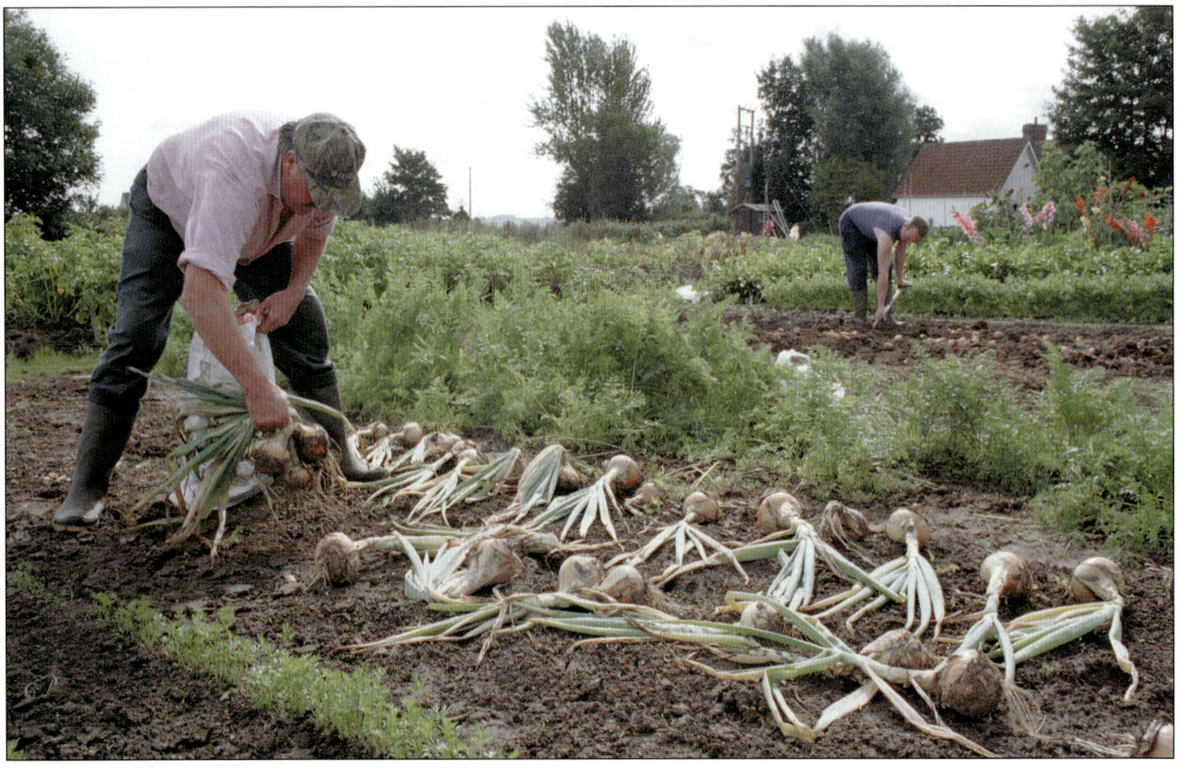

Motorway? What motorway? Just occasionally, Nature likes to show us what things were like in days now gone forever. One morning in late summer, the view across the Dauntsey Vale *(below)* was as marvellous as ever, but a ribbon of mist had seeped up from the river and completely shrouded the M4. Down on the other side of those first trees, it's hard to imagine the main London to the West Country transport route is running left to right. Packed with juggernauts and commuters cursing the mist, and still driving too fast, they are sadly unaware that 50 yards away up the hill, a bright summer's morning is beginning. You'd need a pea-souper to hide the pylons though.

Above: Swans pair for life and these two have made the river south of Lower Seagry their home.

Left: If having pristine gardens isn't enough, the village allotments are a hive of activity through to the late summer and, if your green fingers are in order, provide a good crop.

WITH a lifetime working the land around the village, parents with land up towards Startley, an uncle with land at Seagry Heath and his father before him owning what is now called Trinity Farm - there can be no one still around more important to Seagry's century than **Bill Hayward**. Now in his late 70s, he was born in the village the year his father bought Church Farm in Lower Seagry. After so many years working the land, Bill now takes it easy at the farm still run by his son-in-law John Kingston: Upper Seagry's most important holding, Manor Farm. To say 'times have changed' since Bill milked his first cow would be a cliche to unfairly shroud the monumental changes in village life he has witnessed. But the eyes are still bright as Bill wryly watches newcomers arrive and settle in. "I've seen a few changes, and people always say 'times were harder', but it's because that was true." he said. "When I was a lad, I had to hand-milk five cows before and after school. When we got to be young men, we'd walk with the horses all day, then go out to Chippenham all night and walk home in the early hours. "It was a different community altogether. Nobody went far from their village for anything, everybody stayed pretty local." People used to come in to the farmhouse for their milk every morning, freshly milked minutes earlier. "There was nothing on the roads at these times, every village had its own post office, village shop - it's what city folk think villages are still like, when in fact they've come in and drive to the supermarket miles away for everything."

Bill is thankful his two daughters - he married a nurse from Chippenham - still farm locally. Rosemary and her husband John Kingston still work Manor Farm while Molly has arable land up towards Stanton. "It's funny - my uncle wasn't a fan of arable at all - he was a cattle man through and through - 'horrible' instead of 'arable' he used to call it," recalled Bill.

Much of Bill's generation has gone - either passed away or moved away - but lifelong friend Doug Wiltshire still comes to call every morning to pass the time, just as he has done for the past 50 years. Not much changed in the way of farming life in Seagry for hundreds of years until the final years of the 20th century - in Bill and Doug there remains a window to the past. They remember it how it used to be, now it's changed forever.

When the M4 motorway came to Seagry it brought the modern age slap-bang in the middle of rural Wiltshire. The towns around; Swindon, Chippenham and Malmesbury, became high-tech hubs of the telecommunications age with call centres, IT firms and mobile phone companies setting up just a few miles from **Oscar Rawlings'** home. How many of the executives who scoot past Oscar's cottage on their way to junction 17 would believe that in the last year of the 20th century, they pass a man who has never, ever, in his life before, used a telephone?

He's never had one, wants one, never needed to use one and never felt the need to get one. The information superhighway and the worldwide web are simply a different world from Oscar's simple and content life in the villages of North Wiltshire. The village's oldest resident at 86, he moved to Seagry relatively late in life - just 15 years ago. He's moved twice before and made a slow progression east from his birth place of Castle Combe to Yatton Keynell and then most of his life in Grittleton - two villages west of Seagry. He had a varied working life which included time as a garage mechanic, 30 years in the building trade, as a driver and on the Neeld Estate in Grittleton. He came to Seagry with his wife Ellen to be closer to one of his four children - daughter Joy Selwood. As we talk, he chops logs for the fire and we note how many big cars are racing home from the motorway junction a couple of miles west. "People are different, there's no doubt," he said. "They live faster lives. Nobody's got any time anymore. I'm not so busy now, I don't get up until 9am. In my life, I've had a go at just about everything. But all I know is I didn't get any richer, I just got poorer!"

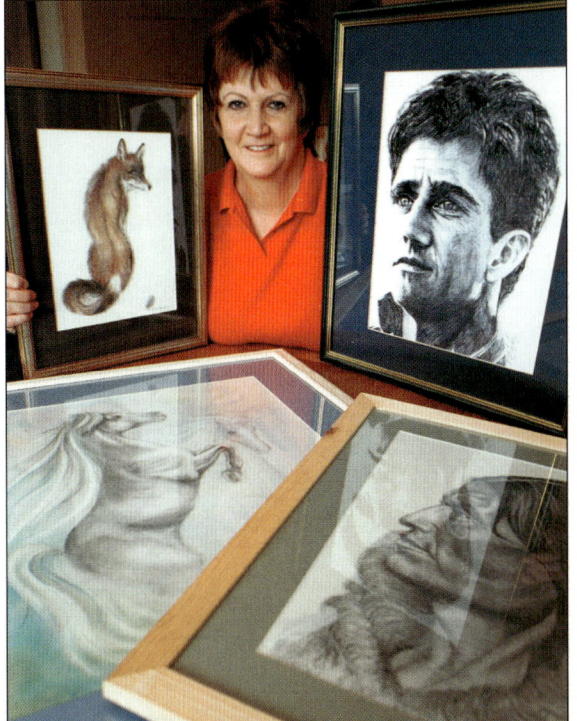

More Seagry folk at work and at play: (clockwise from top left) Paddy Ryan has been caretaker at the village hall for years; Elise Bright celebrated her first birthday on April 1, with smiling parents Tina and Michael; Melanie Newman's a dab hand with flowers; Patrick Head grew up at Seagry House, and now lives with his wife Carol and a one-eyed lawnmower at nearby Oakhill House; the Davies family at Seales Court and finally artist Patricia Douglass' work was exhibited at a gallery in Nailsworth during 1999.

94

95

This page: Everyone loves a good wedding, and Seagry had three very different ones to celebrate. Juliet Milner walked to the church with her father Peter, and returned as Mrs Mark Pelling to be showered with confetti by the Wykehams. David Jackson and Christine de la Riviere (bottom right) married at Chippenham Registry office, while Sam Andrews and Lesley Marshall (bottom left) romantically went to Gretna Green to be wed.

This page: The fading blue sky of a late summer's day on the old gravel pits that are now Somerford Lakes, between Great Somerford and Lower Seagry, fisherman Ian Blackmore could be forgiven for thinking he's the only person in the world.

WHILE Seagry's rector, Rev Guy Oswald, would be the first to admit that the days when every villager went to church every Sunday without fail have gone, reports of the death of the Church of England are more than premature. Anyone writing off the church as a force in the community should come to Seagry, where 1999 saw the continued revival. Many villagers go to church and are involved, it's just that they do it quietly, and the church is still at the heart of village life.

Previous page: Former Seagry resident Mary Lewis came from Sutton Benger to man the checkpoint for the immensely popular annual Wiltshire Historic Churches Bike Ride (bottom right). Cyclists get sponsored to visit as many churches in the county as possible in one day. The late summer warmth also helped the youngsters enjoy the church barbecue, held in September (bottom left). Its primary intention isn't to preach, or even to raise funds for the church, but just to bring the community together for one last evening of summer fun before the nights draw in.

With 110 days left of the second Millennium, villagers answered a call to gather for a histori
Trinity Farm. Rob Biggin brought out a farm tractor, and Paul stood in the front bucket to g
summer that the vi

*ograph. Lower Seagry's picture (above) took place at noon on Sunday, September 12, outside
on needed. Fifty-five residents came outside on what was the last warm day of a mini-Indian
in early September.*

*Three hours later, and the tractor was brought up to the school playing fiel[d
picture, and the tractor's front bucket had to be raised a little higher. It was
an eye for the rows of emp[

*ewis. One hundred and three residents of Upper Seagry turned out for the
imes that organisers thought to inform the police in case any burglars with
d kept an eye on things.*

The rueful look of a man who has made a tough decision. The last picture of dairy cows on Manor Farm, Upper Seagry, *(above)* taken just after John Kingston decided to give up milking at the end of the summer.

It wasn't just a straight business decision, if it was, he'd probably have done it long ago. John Kingston loves cows but milking them for just love and not money took its toll and he simply didn't enjoy it any more.

Now John is content to plough the arable part of Manor Farm (right), and look after 60 or so beef cattle.

He no longer has to get up before the lark every morning - something which Rob Biggin *(right)* still does, even though he might well have gone to bed at four in the morning after travelling back from an overnight farmers' protest.

Rob milks 190 Holsteins and finds it incredible and frustrating that milk is now cheaper to buy in the shops than bottled water: scant reward for a twice-daily ritual which takes two and a half hours each time. Each cow takes just seven minutes to give around 28 litres of milk and 20 cows line up each time. The unending task is the reason for the farmers' weak bargaining position: what else can they do with the milk but sell it at the price they're given?

Autumn

UNLIKE the gradual and unnoticeable transition from spring to summer, everyone knows when autumn begins. It's the first time you need a jumper on all day, when a windy night makes a carpet of leaves in the morning, when a shower of rain makes things cold rather than nice and cool and when you first notice birds weighing down their telegraph wire departure lounges.

Children reluctantly know when the summer ends - it's when they go back to school in the first week of September - although this year saw what used to be called an 'Indian summer', with T-shirt days sneaking well into September. Welcome though those are, the downside is when the chilly winds of autumn do come, there's a sudden change.

But this year things were slightly different. This year, everyone had something to look forward to. The falling leaves meant the village was another step closer to its biggest ever party, on the last night of the century.

Autumn in Seagry is a colourful and lively time. The woods around the village go from green and yellow to all the shades of brown, the hedgerows and woodland floors seem to wake up from their hazy summer slumbers as creatures prepare for the winter ahead in a rush of scurrying activity.

On the land itself, the cows are brought in, the crops are harvested, the barns bulge and creak and the never-ending cycle of seasonal tradition turns another notch once more, with harvest festivals, conker matches and new children arriving at the village school.

Wipe a tear from your eye, mums and dads, because it really is true your babies are all grown up and now don smart new Seagry School jumpers, yet to develop inexplicable holes or to be splashed with paint. With hands strictly on the knees, the new arrivals line up for posterity (above). (Back row, from the left): Robert Brownsell, Rachael King, Naomi Nash, Shaw Roberts, Max Harrop, Louise Harrison and Danielle Clarke. Front row: Sebastian Chater Davies, Verity Clark, James Melia, Mollie Watling, Ben Williams, Emily Lloyd and Rebecca Rose Lewis. They weren't the only new boys and girls: arriving for his first day at Seagry School was new headteacher David Brown (right).

This impromptu and informal whole school photograph was taken on October 11, when all the very little ones had settled in to enjoying a full days work.

STANTON
LOWER SEAGRY
GT. SOMERFORD
TO THE CHURCH
SUTTON BENGER
CHIPPENHAM
STARTLEY
MALMESBURY
THE NEW INN at SEAGRY
FREE HOUSE
GIVE WAY

THE COUNTRYSIDE around Seagry is a delight to walk in throughout the year, but autumn is a magical time.

Villager Mike Collins has devised and described four routes which will take walkers on strolls around both Upper and Lower Seagry. All walks will take between an hour and an hour-and-a-half and start and finish, rather conveniently, at the New Inn.

The map showing the routes is overleaf, and here's Mike's guide to what to look out for on the way.

Blue Route (north) *A pleasant selection of paths encompassing Oak Hill Wood and Seagry Wood via field tracks and local lanes to Startley before returning to Seagry.*

Oak Hill Wood has a profusion of bluebells, primroses and wood anemones in the springtime which are quite accessible from the lane and paths. Wildlife to look for especially are buzzards (with their distinctive 'mewing' call), foxes, badgers and roe deer. The main track though the woods can be muddy in places but is a pleasant green lane from woods to Startley. See if you can spot the rowan trees (mountain ashes) in Seagry Wood.

Orange Route (west) *A stroll to the west of the village which brushes the motorway but is a million miles from contraflows and fast lanes.*

A choice of tracks through Ellwood leading southerly to exit woods near a stone pillared gateway into typical English parkland. You then head towards the motorway along 18th and 19th century coach tracks which used to be lined with daffodils, and some still remain. On the track from the motorway bridge are two ponds frequented by dragonflies. Other wildlife includes roe deer, buzzards and hares. If you are lucky, flora rhododendrons, bluebells and primroses can be seen in season.

Pink Route (south) *A mixture of lane, hard track and field tracks passing close to a Cotswold stone farmhouse and farm at Hardinge.*

The track meanders through a pleasant valley of tree lined fields. Please close the farm gates! A left turn at the M4 motorway leads to another hard track to Seagry Hill. On this track in May and June wild orchids can be found, pyramid and bee orchids (don't pick, just look!). Other flora in season are teasels, hips and haws, lady smock and red campion. Fauna includes roe deer, buzzards and badgers. The return to the New Inn gives a leisurely view of most of the village of Upper Seagry.

Yellow Route (east) *A walk down the main street to Manor Farm to take up the footpath through the fields and hedgerows to Seagry Mill House on the River Avon Weir.*

The Old Mill pond can be seen on the right hand side of the river crossing. Then, by footpath towards Lower Seagry to the village church and the Tithe Barn at Church Farm. Returning to Upper Seagry you will pass the Old Seagry School House. Then the New Inn via Five Thorns Lane. Wildlife to look out for includes swans, moorhens, ducks, herons and kingfishers (if you

are lucky) on the River Avon. Flora includes willows, reeds, various wild flowers in season, and the sedges that gives Seagry its old Saxon name.
Previous page: The Knoll in autumn. Left: Seagry youngsters enjoy Oak Hill Wood. Above: Some still get around with old modes of transport, this lady is well known in the Malmesbury area.
Insert pictures on the map overleaf (clockwise from top): The place to start; the signs to follow; a stile leads down the side of Manor Farm house and guide author Mike Collins.

108

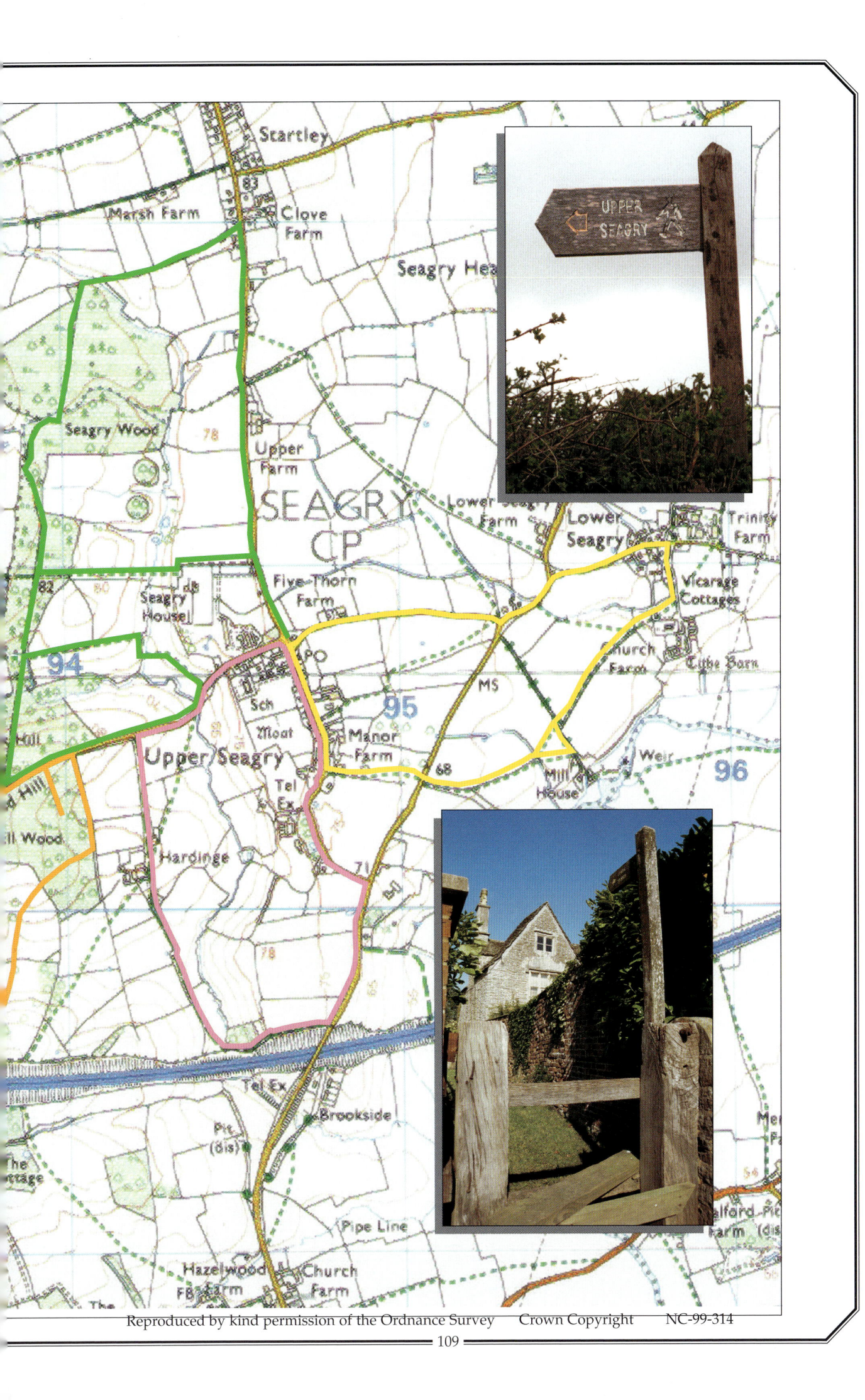

Reproduced by kind permission of the Ordnance Survey   Crown Copyright   NC-99-314

109

Known as the oldest Methodist chapel in the county, it was erected in 1825 by two brothers, George and Cornelius Carey.

The congregation meet every other Sunday afternoon *(bottom picture)*, and the highlight in the calendar is the harvest festival, preached by the Rev. R. Enticott *(right)* where flowers, home-made and home grown produce create a colourful sight to the interior of the chapel. The keyholder of the chapel is Ellen Rawlings *(below)*, a keen member of the Methodist Chapel congregation, and who lives next door.

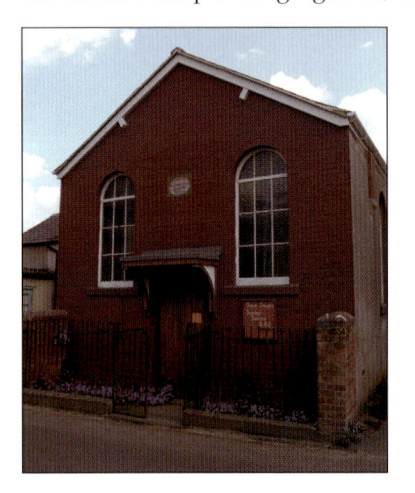

The Courtyard from the west side of Seagry

OCTOBER saw the young and the young-at-heart scouring the woodland floor, collecting conkers and avidly polishing and practising for Seagry's annual conker tournament *(right)*.

Each year the residents of the aptly-named The Chestnuts, Tony and Pat Kay, invite the school to simply come and play conkers in their front garden. It makes a wonderful spectacle which, as the morning progresses, becomes a tense and hard-fought battle.

In a sport that's as old as the Vale itself, many old wives' tales promise to improve the battle-hardiness of your champion conker, although baking them hard is strictly forbidden.

The Chestnuts was also the scene of a remarkable meeting *(below left)*. All the way from Australia, a descendant of Robert Hollis, the man who originally built The Chestnuts back in 1700, returned to retrace his family tree. Within a couple of days of discovering he had an ancestor called Robert Hollis, he found himself sitting in the very rooms the man built and would have sat in. The couple were warmly welcomed at The Chestnuts and given the grand tour.

Above: James Hatherall and Claire Gardner's battle attracted a crowd. Below: James again, this time taking on Matthew Maloney.

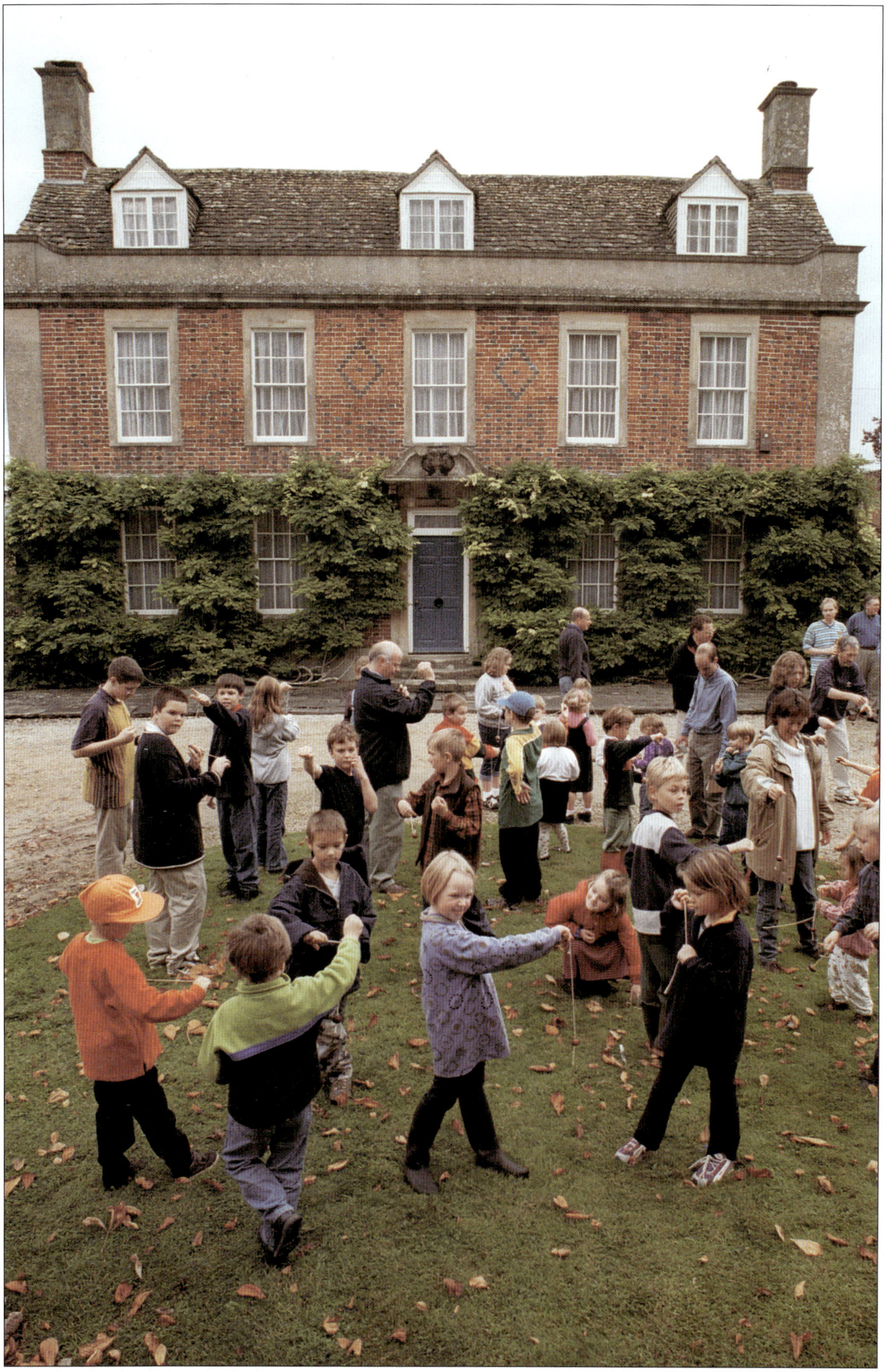

The weird and wonderful world of Royston Ball, Seagry resident and collector of motor memorabilia. Royston has two Lanchesters, which even Doug Wiltshire can't remember being new. And his garage is packed to the very rafters with a myriad of posters, pumps and paraphernalia of a time when cars were a luxury and one driving through Seagry would have had children chasing it.

No need for young Reece Clark to pretend he's aboard a steam traction engine, the legacy of his great-grandfather's life as an engine contractor provides the best play apparatus a small boy could possibly want.

The engine toured the farms of North Wiltshire providing a mobile threshing machine in the days before combine harvesters and the like.

This particular engine has been in the family for 32 years, and used to do a lot of touring the various shows and steam rallies, although nowadays spends more time in graceful retirement in Seagry.

Alastair's father Graham, standing at the back, remembers when this particular engine earned its keep. Other villagers get around in style - Phil Arnold in his classic TR4, and Trinity Farm provides all the space when Bertie Wykeham, David Biggin and his cousin, Edward Winter need to kick up the dirt on board their scrambling bikes.

Autumn saw something new in Seagry, and as the Millennium approached, it seemed fitting that this bright new organisation combined the church and young people.

There had been youth clubs in the village before. In unsophisticated days before the lure of computer games, TV and the world wide web, youngsters in Seagry met to play simple things like table tennis and football, and go on camping trips organised by people like Dermo Selwood.

But numbers and enthusiasm dwindled until something called Rock Solid@Seagry came along.

With a 'hip' new name and image and its own website, the children all came back, even though common 'yoof' thinking has it that a Church Youth Club isn't the coolest thing in the world.

The 11-14 year-olds follow a formula produced by a church group called Youth for Christ, which also provides the materials, games and topics.

"It is a Christian thing, but they are not thumped over the head with a big black bible every time," explained administrator David Brown (the church's David Brown, not his headteacher namesake).

"They're kids and they want to have fun. There is a 'serious' spot in the middle, but it's no more than ten minutes."

The group began at the end of September and meet every Thursday evening in the village hall during term time.

The group follow a three-year programme which rotates as the children pass through.

Youngsters are very fortunate in Seagry to have five youth workers in the immediate area - Phil and Claire Simmonds, Katie and Morgan Brown and Simon Lock - while David Brown takes a back seat. "My kids go, but I've got grey hair, so I'm afraid I'm not cool."

Organisers hope they've struck the balance right, and within months their work paid off. Some Rock Solid members joined one of the Christmas services at the church with readings and a sketch.

In theory, if you attended the Midnight Mass Christmas Eve service at Seagry church, were the worse for a little festive cheer and became unruly, *David Brown* could arrest you.

For his remit as one of two churchwardens still contains un-repealed medieval powers to administer law and order inside God's house in Seagry. But the father-of-two wouldn't dare consider it, and nor, he's sure would senior church warden Gordon Knapp, who's never used those powers in 40 years of wardening. This peaceful man has an air of tranquil contentment that comes from someone who works from a home he loves.

The family - wife Claire and daughters 14-year-old Naomi and 12-year-old Hayley - moved to Lower Seagry in the summer of 1991 from the suburbs of Chippenham. They were looking for a cottage in the country off the beaten track and fell in love with their home despite it needing what estate agents describe as 'attention'. Six years ago, David moved his IT sales consultant's work to an office in the attic and now commutes up a ladder instead of in his car. "You have to be disciplined to work from home, and it helps if you have a dedicated office separate from home life," he said. "It means you can work more hours and saves money in the long run. It also means you can leave lots of paperwork until after the children are in bed and come back up here, instead of working late in the office and missing them entirely."

The last weeks of 1999 saw David take a decision to switch to working more part-time, to devote more time to working for the community. "I can't afford to give up work totally, but now I do have that flexibility to choose what I do and when I do it." Work inside the church organisation takes up much of his time. During the last year of the century he also embarked on a training course to be a lay reader. He is one of the church's representatives on the school's board of governors and goes in to help out from time to time, especially with assemblies. The last few months also saw him instrumental in setting up Rock Solid @Seagry, and he and Claire became regional advisors for North Wiltshire with the church initiative Alpha courses. Other church functions like September's barbecue, carol singing and cheese and wine evenings had input from David, who sees it as essential that the church is pro-active in the community, rather than staying within the thick walls of the church. "I regard the church as a group of people rather than a building. The church is fine for traditional services, but we shouldn't expect them to come to our church, we should be there where they are."

STAND pretty much anywhere in Upper Seagry and you're no more than a few feet from farmland, and that land is probably owned by *Robert Dickinson*, Seagry's senior figure in the farming community. His father moved to the village in 1939 and bought 40 acres of paddock, and since then he and later Robert have 'tried to buy a bit here and there every year'. They've succeeded and now the Dickinson's farm, which is actually based up the road in Startley, covers 200 acres. "Land doesn't lose its value - they don't make it anymore," he said.

Most of the land is arable - the Dickinsons got out of dairying a long time before everyone else and now planting and harvesting give an order to the seasons. In 1999 the spring arrived on time and everything was in the ground by the end of March. Robert grew up in Seagry, went to the local schools and has never considered living anywhere else. But the main passion in his life isn't planting schedules, MAFF forms and combine engines, it's horses. A winning jockey in younger years, Robert was heavily involved in the famous family training business with his Seagry pasture and TLC. Once, five Dickinson horses nabbed the first five positions in the Cheltenham Gold Cup, a feat you can't imagine being repeated.

Robert and his wife Lucy take perhaps the most pride in their two daughters, who are continuing the family passion for all things equestrian. Raised in the saddle, Sophie and Jane both regularly represent Britain in dressage and combined competitions. This year, Sophie travelled to New York and Switzerland to compete at the highest level. Meanwhile, back on the paddocks of Seagry, Robert is still turning out top quality horses. He has high hopes for the two foals pictured by Paul in the spring. There's something about Seagry and horses.

THE penultimate meeting of Seagry Parish Council in the village hall in September. While MPs in parliament quickly learnt the technique of 'doughnuting' - cramming together to trick TV viewers into thinking their benches are packed, Seagry's politicians are used to it. Apart from those pictured above *(from the left: Nobby Lewis, chairman; Mary Kemp, parish clerk; parish councillors Andrew Ball, Patrick Head and John Kingston with district councillor Peter Greene)*, there's precisely no one else in the audience, no members of the electorate. There must have been something good on telly that evening. Apart from regular planning applications and letters urging a crackdown on speeding drivers, Seagry Parish Council made two major undertakings in 1999. The first was to invite other villagers to stand for election in May. "None were received, indicating the village's satisfaction with the existing team!" said parish clerk Mary Kemp. These councillors will now remain in office for a further four years.

"During 1999 it was also agreed that the council should become the Trustees of the Recreation Ground, thereby becoming responsible for the hire and maintenance of the playing fields and the playground." Seagry's taxpayers are, I'm sure, pleased their money isn't wasted on a table for the chairman and clerk which, extravagantly, has all its legs the same length. Folded-up cardboard will do just as well - for free.

Winter

THERE was little talk of doom in Seagry as the second millennium entered its final season. It's a community still close to nature, the land and the seasons. Everyone knew that the Millennium Bug and the impending end of the world or civilisation as we knew it wouldn't stop the frost being followed by the spring in the year 2000.

Winter crept up unnoticed during October and November then, suddenly, a week before Christmas, it started to snow. It only snowed for an afternoon, that night and then again the following afternoon, but it was cold and clear enough to stay on the ground a good week or so.

Far from sending people shivering to their central heating thermostats or their log piles, it seemed to lift everyone's spirits. It was a good three or four years since snow had fallen, settled and stuck, and with a fortnight to go before the big New Year - a historic moment which everyone had looked forward to all their lives - it certainly got everyone in the festive mood.

Compared to the big cities, Seagry's Millennium celebrations were quiet and reserved. Much centered around the church. After all, mankind wasn't only celebrating a new year number with three zeros in it, but the 2,000th birthday of Jesus. While much of the nation forgot, Seagry seemed to remember.

So it was a time more for reflection and hope than for hedonism. The winter was like any other with its own winter rituals. But with the Millennium and the snow that preceded it, this winter was one of the most magical.

Bonfire night. People in Seagry, like virtually every culture in the world, have had a festival of light of some sort to mark the onset of the dark winter for centuries if not millennia.

That our's has a tale of 17th century coup-stopping is by the by. The point is to light up the dark evenings, clear out all the junk and get together as a community to mark the time when it's dark as you get up and it's dark before tea. Some days it stays twilight.

So wood was collected, a bonfire built - by Dermo Selwood, who else? - and word went round the pub that people should bring their own fireworks to the rec.

It wasn't an official and organised display, just the village coming together in an ad hoc manner.

Above: Co-organiser Nobby Lewis, silhouetted Andy Capp-style against the flames, while Kyle Stallard (left) draws circles with a sparkler.

For some in a village community, the most momentous change possible comes when the man in charge of the village's beer supply changes. And in 1999, not only did the village headteacher hang up his marking pen, but so did David Lock, who had run the New Inn for over 11 years.

Dave moved to the pub with his wife Jacqueline in 1988, and had to start from scratch. The pub had been an empty shell for 18 months, and within months they'd started a successful pub/restaurant business. The couple enjoyed many happy years behind the bar, and were much-loved in the village. Always willing to help the community, the couple managed to keep a healthy balance between the commercial food side of the business, and the notion of the village pub at the heart of village life. Many a committee, council meeting, club and work detail was sorted out in the pub which the Locks tried to keep as a traditional village inn.

But it wasn't a quiet life: "It's a myth when people say they're going to take it easy and run a village pub, I've never worked so hard in my life," said Dave. 'In the end, we were getting tired and the Stones came along and twisted our arms. I'm now at 53 years of age and I am taking it easy. After 11 years, the place needs new faces and new ideas. The norm is to run a pub for five years."

The new faces arrived on November 8th. Mike and Rosey Stone had run several pubs in the Chippenham area, and like their predecessors had worked in the business for decades, most recently at the bustling Little George pub in the centre of Chippenham.

"What attracted us was the pub itself. We'd been past it, but never inside, and it was lovely," said Mike. "We wanted a more sedate life - there were too many youngsters at the Little George."

Regulars bade a fond farewell to Dave and Jacqui and gave a warm welcome to Mike and Rosey, who tinkered rather than made any drastic changes. With so many village pubs under threat, Seagry folk were relieved their inn would continue to thrive in the new century.

It really was too good to miss, and even those who hate the sheer coldness and wetness of it couldn't help but admire the beauty of their village blanketed in white. With two weeks before predicted Millennium meltdown, it was as if Mother Nature was reminding us she is the boss and not a computer. Paul Stallard was out using film like it was going out of fashion. Here's the church *(above)*, Wood Lane west of Upper Seagry *(below left)*, Chestnut Lodge and a view across the fields near Seagry Woods *(below right)* and finally *(opposite page, top)* the entrance to Hardinge Farm Lane.

122

(*Below*): Never has a road sign been more accurate, this one entering Upper Seagry from Five Thorns Lane. There's a downside to living two miles from the nearest main road. When it snows, the gritting lorries and snowploughs don't come. While many 'incomers' from the towns wondered how they could traverse these snowbound and icy roads across North Wiltshire, and wrote to the council to complain, older folk smiled. They remember when the village would be cut off for weeks.

The Christmas spirit embodied in a show of illuminations. It doesn't matter if it's grand old Seagry House *(above)*, or a former council house at Broadleaze *(below)* they all impress with stunning lights. The illuminated Christmas tree stands outside the east wing of Seagry House, while there's a fair deal of competition on Broadleaze for the best, most striking or wittiest Christmas display. The electricity bills don't come until the spring. *(Right) The nativity play at Seagry Playgroup captures the real meaning of Christmas.*

125

The church's Christmas: Rev. Oswald leads the singing amid smiling faces in the warmth of a carol singing evening at Seagry House; a nativity service at the church and the church's charming crib display, complete with proportionately huge pieces of straw.

So this is it. New Year's Eve 1999 in Seagry was a simple, honest, unassumingly raucous affair with revellers in the pub as well as at two parties. 'Mr Chairman', Nobby Lewis (right) and other helpers organised an unofficial village do in the village hall, while Rob and Clare Clilverd celebrated not only the turn of the Millennium, but also Clare's 40th birthday the day before with a big bash at home.

No one can quite remember if the hat on Nobby's head is the same one on Clare's head later in the evening. It was a good night.

Acknowledgements

We would like to express our thanks to the many people mentioned in the book for their kindness in helping us to collect material for it. In addition to those whose names appear in the text, our special thanks go to the following: Derek and Mary Kemp, Peter and Aino Milner, Keith and Anthea Lanning, Mike and Margaret Collins, Derek (Dermo) and Joy Selwood, Richard Vivash, Richard Bridge, Jim Stent, Bill Cardno, Rosemary Kingston, Michael (Nobby) Lewis, Debbie Short, Rob and Clare Clilverd, Richard Maugham, Maggie Scanlan, Mike and Rosey Stone, David Brown (both of them!), Nick Janes, Ian Blackmore, Michael Bright, Nick Wykeham, Patrick Head, James York Moore, Rev. Guy Oswald, Alun Phillips, Louise Jones, Chris and Claire McGine, Chris Chard, Sally Tregoning, Richard Wintle, Mark Stallard, Nick Flexon-Cook, Andy Nurden, Andy James, Bob Sparrow, Roy Waine, Cynthia Poole, Anne Turner, Mick Canty, Erwin Chwistek, Geoffrey Gunn, John Chandler, Ordnance Survey, The Millennium Festival Awards For All Programme, North Wiltshire District Council, Wilts. & Gloucestershire Standard, Western Daily Press and of course our wives, Kathie and Clare.

...y Brown year 4
Seagrys Best Book ever
Helena Baker class 2 Age 7
super snaps
peony class 2 7 Seagry expressions
Seagrys Book photograph 200...
Robynne Jade Hinkley 7 class?
Photographs Book in Seagry.
Alice Bell year 3 class 3
Seagry Beast oWBain 2000
year 4 Samantha Jane Fellows
Seagrys book 2000
Benedict Dart year 4
Grat things about seagry
Hugh Seagry log 2000 year 3
Katie T. year 4
Seagrys Book of P... Baker class 2 Age 7
5
SEAG...
Rosie Everett class 2 age ...
Katie Ryan